Of Sinks
&
Pulpits

Elizabeth Sutherland

1

First Published in Great Britain
by
For the Right Reasons
60 Grant Street, Inverness, IV3 8BS
fortherightreasons@rocketmail.com
Changing lives through Enterprise

Cover design by Kevin Swanson

ISBN: 978-1-905787-71-5

Also by Elizabeth Sutherland:
The Black Isle, (nf) 1972; Lent Term (f) 1973; The Seer of Kintail
(f) 1974; Hannah Hereafter, (f) 1976; The Eye of God (f) 1977;
The Prophecies of the Brahan Seer (edit) (nf) 1977; The Weeping
Tree (f) 1980; Ravens and Rain (nf) 1985; The Gold Key and the
Green Life (edit)(nf) 1986; In Search of the Picts (nf) 1994; The
Pictish Trail (nf) 1996; The Five Euphemias (nf) 1997; Lydia,
Wife of Hugh Miller of Cromarty (b) 2002; The Bird of Truth (f)
2006; Boniface, Bishops and Bonfires (nf) 2010; Amendment of
Life (f) 2010; Children of God (nf) 2010 One Of The Good Guys
(nf) 2012

Contact For The Right Reasons to order any of the above books.

Of Sinks and Pulpits

The Parish Years
1944-1982

Foreword

How easy it is to look back from the knowledge and security of old age and speak for that person who was once young, that flibbertigibbet who was once me. Thus I can say with a certain amount of confidence and no one to argue the point that I would have followed in my late father's footsteps and become a priest in the Scottish Episcopal Church if such a thing as the ordination of women had been thinkable in the 1940s. Truthfully, at the time, it never crossed my mind. However, judging from my subsequent choices in life that, at the time, seemed haphazard, instinctive and mostly unconsidered, I can see now that they could all be viewed as substitutes for what I would have chosen, or, hopefully been called to become, had it not been for the fact that I was born female. (Yes, and glad to be. At no stage in my life, had I been given a choice, would I have chosen to be male.)

But you shall be the judge. The only fact in my early life that I can be sure of is this: I wanted to write which is not quite the same as wanting to become 'a writer'. I never thought of myself in the same profession as an Austen or a Bronte. All we had in common was the fact that we were daughters of clergymen. I knew for certain from the age of five that I wanted to write, I did write, and, eighty plus years on, that ambition has never changed.

I must also confess to you now, before you read another word, that my life has not been adventurous, exciting, salacious or even difficult, so if that is what you are looking for in a memoir then you had better put this book aside and read Bear Grylls (where did that name come from?) or Janice Galloway (who knows exactly how to write a memoir) or Richard Holloway (whose faith journey is enthralling). Nor am I sure where to start…

In the train, perhaps, leaving Kinross Junction for Edinburgh University. According to my diary, the train was crowded with service personnel because this was 1944, Monday 9 October to be precise, and it was still war time.

I - it's no use - I cannot write this memoir of my middle years, the parish years, from the personal pronoun because the person I was so long ago seems to have little connection to the person I am now. I felt the same in the memoir of my childhood (*Children of God*) and my perceptions have not changed. I cannot believe that the teenager in the blue coat and skirt in the smoky railway carriage was once me. It has to be 'she'.

Chapter One

Digs and Money

Betty was feeling rich, her handbag full of half-crowns given to her by Annie and the Kirkwoods and all the farm folk. She had found accepting these tips a little embarrassing because she was no longer a schoolgirl but at the same time she was grovellingly grateful for their generosity and particularly for the pound note generously handed to her by Aunt Nell. Her beautiful pigskin handbag was new and cost a princely six guineas. Her mother had bought it for her in Dundee the previous week. She was wearing her best coat and skirt, a light blue-flecked tweed which because it was a little soft stretched too easily and sagged a bit around the bottom. Her hair which had been permed the previous week - half a perm, in fact, which only curled the ends and was thus a lot cheaper than the full head - had already gone a little frizzy. Her hair was always a problem, too fine, too inclined to go greasy, hard to manage, though, secretly, she quite liked its colour, dark and glossy brown. Pity about the frizzy ends. She would have to use curlers every night to keep them under control and she hated sleeping in curlers.

Outwardly she was calm, her heavy leather suitcase dragging from one arm, the pigskin bag clutched in the other. Eighteen - just - was, after all, grown up more or less, and she was on her way to Edinburgh University to read Social Science. Inwardly she was excited, nervous, happy, terrified, shy and over-confident all at the same time. There were four RAF pilots in her compartment. She felt bold enough to flirt a little. Their friendliness was surely a good omen.

At Waverley station she caught a tram out to Colinton. Her right arm felt twice its usual length by the time she had reached No 12 Beech Avenue, dumped the case on the doorstep and rung the bell.

She had obstinately refused to take one of the rooms offered to her by the university in the new-ish hall of residence at East Suffolk Road. Six and a half years of boarding school had been enough. She wanted to be free, though she was not exactly sure what freedom meant. Her mother was equally sure that she was too young and certainly too inexperienced to be let loose in an Edinburgh overflowing with soldiers on leave from all the free countries, particularly the predatory Americans, stationed in Princes Street, so a compromise had been reached: Beech Avenue

Beech Avenue was a terrace of small stone houses, half houses really, in a cul-se-sac facing a small park with tennis courts at the far end. After the dark and chilly vastness of Shanwell it seemed like a dolls' house, bright, warm, cosy. The living room to the left of the staircase with its bay window and gas fire was dominated by the obligatory three-piece suite of sofa and two armchairs covered in chintz. Leading out of it, the small dining room had space for a sideboard and the precious French-polished table covered at all times with green baize and a starched white tablecloth. Behind that was the kitchen where Betty was expected to take her fair share of cooking and washing up. No hardship this for the cooker was gas, and a joy to use after the temperamental black kitchen range at Shanwell. She learned how to make a roux sauce with no lumps for which she was to be grateful to her hostess (you couldn't call Mrs C a landlady) for the rest of her life.

Upstairs were three bedrooms, or rather two bedrooms and a box-room which was to be hers. Its smallness did not upset her in the least. All the easier to keep tidy was her first thought. How wrong she was. Betty could not be tidy in a cupboard. But she was not excused. On mornings without lectures she was presented with a brush and pan and duster or the large loud hoover and shown exactly what to do. Afterwards her work was inspected critically. Mrs C did her best to teach her to be tidy.

For the year she lived in Beech Avenue she never entered either of the other two bedrooms but assumed that Mrs C shared the front room with the bay window with her twelve-year old daughter, Jean, and that ten-year old Bobby was next door to her with the bathroom between. She had no idea where the various uncles and cousins stayed when they visited. Uncle John, frail and crotchety, was more or less a fixture that first term. Nor did she give it much thought.

6

Mrs C was the sister of a friend of her mother who lived near Kinross. She let it be known that Mrs C, twice widowed, was hard-up and looking for a student lodger. Mother saw it as the perfect solution, and so, in many ways, it was. Mrs C was strict but warm-hearted, cooked well and taught Betty the rudiments of housekeeping. Jean and Bobby were nice children. She helped Jean with her maths home work, managing to conceal the fact that she knew a great deal less than Jean about how to solve problems, and played endless board games with Bobby. There was a down side however. Everything that Betty did, everyone she met, every dance she attended, was noted and reported by Mrs C to her sister, who, with embellishments, passed on the information to Mother.

So freedom was illusory. 12 Beech Avenue was like home only smaller. Jean and Bobby became younger siblings and Mrs C kept a strict eye on her social life, expected her home by 10 30 pm unless she had been warned to the contrary. Mrs C made one mistake, however. In an expansive mood, she suggested to Betty that she might like to bring her friends in for a cup of tea after a night out at the cinema or the Caledonian dance hall. So she did.

It was an expensive mistake. By the time Betty came in with her friend of the moment (always male) Mrs C and the children were in bed. Cups of tea were duly made, the gas fire relit and it stayed on until the friend left which might have been as late as 1 am.

'What time did Hugo leave?' Jean would ask curiously at breakfast. Hugo was her first boy friend.

'I've no idea,' Betty would reply airily reaching for the marmalade.

'What were you doing all that time?' Jean would ask curiously.

'Nothing,' she answered carelessly.

Mrs C also said nothing, but she knew, of course she knew. Her bedroom was immediately above the sitting room, but, bless her, she said nothing. She had been young herself and she had had two husbands, but she said nothing.

Betty swore to herself that next time she would not be so late, but she always was.

Finally Mrs C put her foot down. Hugo was no longer welcome which was a great relief to Betty. She had been trying to dump him for weeks. By this time she had found Ben.

As the term progressed so her evenings became busier. Part of the Social Science Certificate course was work experience, and the Girls Youth Club she attended in the Pleasance occupied two nights in the week. The University Choir another evening, sometimes two, as she was in the small choir which contributed to regular concerts, and, as often as possible, the cinema, which would have been every free night had she been able to afford it.

Her allowance was £12 10/ a quarter. Tram fares to the Old Quad and train fares home to Shanwell, daily lunches and morning coffees, cigarettes, cosmetics and sanitary towels stretched that income to the limit. Every Monday morning, she called in at the head branch of the Commercial Bank in George Street, a vast echoing cathedral of a building and solemnly cashed her weekly cheque for a pound (a ten shilling note and the rest in change for the trams). The teller was always the same venerable, white-haired old gentleman who got to know her over the months. On one occasion she had tried to cash a cheque for two pounds (she had seen a dirndl skirt that she coveted costing ten shillings and sixpence) and he had looked at her over the counter and given her a word of warning. 'What happens at the end of the quarter and you have no money left in your account?' he asked her sternly. She had blushed with embarrassment and hung her head. Reluctantly he had counted the money out. She never bought that dirndl skirt, but the money went anyhow.

Lunches were a big item. Sometimes she ate in the Women's Union where the food was subsidised and she met her new girl friends but it was far more fun to go out. The *Overseas Club* in Princes Street cost a princely half-a-crown for a three-course lunch so was only possible when someone else paid. *The Three Tuns* on the High Street cost one and sixpence for soup, pie and beans and a slice of apple tart and custard, a real find. The High Street had lots of little eating-places and over her two years at varsity she probably sampled them all. *Jenners* in Princes Street was nicest because of their delicious, hot, vanilla soufflé puddings.

Mother always took her to *Jenners* where she had an account. Oh dear, that account. Betty had developed a passion for cosmetics, Elizabeth Arden, to be precise. Surely Mother wouldn't mind if she tried out that new lipstick... Would she even notice? Of course Mother noticed. It was still wartime. She was exceedingly hard up. Her widow's pension from the church amounted to £52 a year and her stocks and shares were at their lowest yield. She had two daughters still at boarding school and Betty on the loose in Edinburgh. Of course she noticed and of course Betty knew she shouldn't charge even a lipstick to the account, but sometimes the temptation was too great.

Cigarettes were a necessary item. She had started smoking clandestinely in the bathing huts at school and in spite of Mother pleading with her not to begin, she never took her advice seriously. Mother herself smoked, Annie smoked, Aunt Nell smoked, most of her friends smoked, nearly everyone she knew smoked. By the time she got to varsity she was addicted. Paying for them was another matter. *Wills Woodbines* in their green packets were cheapest but fairly foul. *Players Weights* were preferable, smaller than *Players Navy Cut* and milder than those throat-rasping *Wills Goldflake*. A pink packet of *Passing Cloud* with its Turkish flavour was an exotic luxury she could seldom afford, and, truth to tell, did not much like. Hugo favoured *Balkan Sobranie* which were slightly sick-making. Coloured cigarettes with gold tips called *Du Maurier* were her favourite, but far too expensive. She took to using a short black cigarette holder which made her feel sophisticated, until she lost it.

Sometimes when her money had run out she was known, with others, to go round the tables at Medical Martins - the coffee shop opposite the grand entrance to the Old Quad patronised by students - and collect the stubs out of the ashtrays. She would then remove the remaining tobacco and stuff it with a sliver of paper in into a neat little machine. She never much cared for roll-ups, these least of all, but sometimes needs must. She would rather do without food than cigarettes.

The cinema was another necessity. She would have gone as often as the programmes changed no matter what was on show, no matter who was starring, if she had had enough time and money. That first term she managed eleven films, five concerts, five operas including two D'Oyly Carte operettas, four plays acted by the Wilson Barrett Repertory Company and one variety show at the Empire starring Vera Lynn, who sang beautifully but was surprisingly plain. Her godfather took her to *La Boheme* at which she wept buckets but she sat in the Gods at the Kings Theatre at one and six a ticket for *Cosi van Tutti* and *Gianni Schicchi*.

The cinema, however, was her first love. Laurence Olivier's Mr Darcy appeared that autumn, and Basil Rathbone in the *Mask of Zorro*, was another favourite. *The Song of Bernadette* with Jennifer Jones was followed by *Lost in a Harem* with Abbott and Costello. She wasn't exactly discriminating. Mostly her current boyfriend paid. So many of the male students at varsity (always known as 'boys') were ex-service men who had been wounded and discharged. They had small pensions and could afford it.

Another expense was the music room at *Methven and Simpson* in Princes Street. Betty had studied piano since she had been six years old, and, although she was inaccurate, (the same with typing), and lost her nerve completely whenever she had to perform in public, she loved to play and sing to herself. She had a book of Beethoven Sonatas and Chopin Preludes and Nocturnes and also one of Scottish songs which had belonged to her grandmother, so she would play and sing *Leezie Lindsay* or *Ae Fond Kiss* (her favourite), over and over again in one of the sound-proof closets which cost half-a-crown an hour to hire, hearing, no doubt, only what she wanted to hear.

Although it cost her nothing in cash, time, too, had to be found for writing. She had already bought a fat notebook with ruled lines and she knew exactly how she was going to use it. This was to be her first attempt at a full-length novel. It would be about a girl from the Pleasance, where Betty assisted in a youth club, how she coped with poverty and finally escaped. Her name was Winnie, she lived in 6 Beaumont Crescent and she had five younger brothers. Betty wrote three chapters before realising that she knew nothing about life in the Pleasance. The more she worked with the girls the less she understood their lives. After those three chapters she laid the notebook aside. She was aware of her own ignorance and inadequacy that could only be cured by experience. She never went back to that novel.

Digs at Beech Terrace ended after three terms. It was a mutual and amicable parting. Mrs C's Uncle John was to become a permanent fixture and therefore Bobby was to have the box room. Meanwhile Betty found herself somewhere else.

Part of her Social Science course involved practical work in the long summer holidays. During that first summer term she had to spend four weeks with the Council of Social Service, a voluntary organisation run by (it seemed) several very small, very elderly and very kind old ladies. Sometimes she accompanied one of the old ladies on her visits to various needy souls; sometimes she was sent out on her own.

These solo visits tended to be to people living in the top flats of tenement blocks in the days before lifts. At the age of eighteen, eight or ten flights of stone stairs presented no problems and so that was why she ended up on her own in the top flat of a tenement block in quiet respectable East Preston Street about two miles up the road from the Old Quad.

Mrs H had requested a visit from the Council of Social Service. Recently widowed from her husband whom she always called 'the musician', she found herself lonely. Her son, Jimmy, a soldier in Europe, thought maybe a lodger might be the answer. She had approached the CSS for help in finding someone suitable. Betty was shown over the accommodation which included a spacious sitting room crammed with old-fashioned furniture and a large bay window with a table and aspidistra in a pot. The room also contained two violins, a trumpet and a banjo all hanging on the wall, and, *mirabile dictu,* there was also an upright piano with a metronome on top. 'The musician' had not only been organist in a large city church but also a piano teacher.

Adjoining the sitting-room, was a small bedroom with a single bed, a wardrobe and a washstand with a bowl and jug. The downside, Mrs H explained anxiously, was no bathroom. Weighed against the piano, the two rooms and Mrs H's timid suggestion of 25 shilling a week all found, this still seemed like the bargain of the century (Mrs C had charged 30/-.) Fortunately there was a lavatory, a small dark poky place which had at one time been the hall cupboard. For washing, Mrs H made do with the kitchen sink.

'Would I do?' Betty asked on the spur of the moment. It was not exactly professional behaviour on Betty's behalf, but, bless her, Mrs H's face had not fallen, nor had it exactly lit up. She would have to think about it and discuss it with her daughter-in-law who always visited on Sundays. Perhaps Miss Graeme would like to come to tea on Sunday and meet Mrs Jimmy? Indeed she would.

Mrs Jimmy was small, bespectacled and clever. She worked for an accountant. 'We would have liked Mother to come to us, but she prefers to stay here,' she explained after she had posed some searching questions and asked for a reference. 'Are you sure this is what you're really looking for?' she asked a little doubtfully. 'Won't you find it a little'...she hesitated, '...quiet?'

Betty who was wolfing down a spectacularly lavish tea assured her that it was exactly what she was looking for, so it was arranged that she would move in the day before the autumn term started in early October.

Her own mother was equally doubtful. 'But we don't know anything about her,' she said anxiously, 'and how on earth will you manage without a bathroom?'

'Of course I'll manage,' she replied a little squashingly, and she had been right. Mrs H turned out to be the landlady from heaven. She brought in a can of hot water every morning at seven-thirty for Betty to pour into the china basin on the washstand. Porridge followed by a cooked breakfast was served in the kitchen at eight. High tea was a moveable feast round about six served in her newly acquired sitting room on a spotless white tablecloth with at least three kinds of bought cake, scones and pancakes and a hot meal. Yes of course she could bring back her friends. There was plenty to go round. The only small drawback Betty found was that unless she asked friends to help demolish the cakes and pastries, they turned up every day thereafter until they had all been eaten. Victoria sandwich, delicious on days one, two, even three, developed the consistency of sawdust by the end of the week and Dundee cake did not necessarily improve with age.

12

After she had eaten, the debris was whipped away and the table cleared for her books. Mrs H, without actually spelling it out, saw to it that she finished her essays by excusing her from helping with the washing up. 'I know you students,' she would say encouragingly, 'you'll want to get down to your studying right away.' Ten minutes later she would pop her head round the door on some trivial excuse to make sure that the books were out.

Once a week Mother sent her a postal order for 25 shillings to pay Mrs H. Quite by accident and fairly early on Betty learned that if when she handed over the money in a note and the five shillings in small change rather than two half-crowns Mrs H would slip her the coins. Five extra shillings in her purse! She tried not to make a habit of it but as the months passed it became increasingly hard. She always protested, though not very loudly, and Mrs H always said the same thing, 'It's not the money I'm needing. It's the company.'

She herself was good company, a pretty old lady who liked to hear all the gossip, and Betty found herself spending much of her scant free time in the kitchen chatting. She became in many ways the grandmother that Betty had never known. When Betty gave herself a face pack, she also gave one to Mrs H and they giggled a lot at the sight of their grey-green faces plastered all over like ghosts. She also washed Mrs H's hair in the kitchen sink and set it after she had washed her own. She discussed endlessly her boyfriends and Mrs H talked a lot about 'the musician'. The only time Mrs H was ever cross with her was over a boy friend. Because Mother had made a rule about not seeing John more than once a week, she had taken to going out with other boys when asked. Mrs H had not approved and told her so. Betty had argued what was the harm? Mrs H was firm. It didn't stop Betty, but she learned to keep those other outings strictly to herself.

The lack of a bath soon became evident. What with the Girls Club in the Pleasance and her afternoons at the DHS or in the Juvenile Courts which involved continually hopping on and off trams, strip-washing from the china basin was not enough to keep herself clean. So once a week she was invited to the hall of residence where Jacky, one of her fellow students, had a room, to

13

have a proper bath. One was never enough. It took two to rid herself of the city grime one after another and sometimes a third to soak in.

Otherwise East Preston Street became home from home. Sometimes on Sundays she would accompany Mrs H to tea with Mr and Mrs Jimmy when he was demobbed and they would have a game of cards, or sit out in their patch of garden on deck chairs behind their bungalow in the suburbs. Betty felt part of the family.

Which, of course, was the trouble when the year was over and it was time for her to leave varsity. Mrs H asked her to recommend another student. Sylvia was lovely, desperate for accommodation and Betty thought they would like each other, but she was a third year medical student with no time for face packs or kitchen chats. She lasted for a term.

After nearly seven years at a girls' boarding school and holidays spent in the deep country with Mother, her sisters Bunty and Florence, a younger female cousin, Jill, and Aunt Nell, Betty found the male sex a complete and intriguing mystery. Above all else she wanted to have a boyfriend. but how exactly did one go about finding one? That was the all-absorbing question.

The Students' Union held dances every Friday night. Several of her new friends were going so she agreed to join them. The rectangular room was packed full of young people probably all with the same idea, finding a partner. A four-piece band blared out the pop music of the day, Glen Miller mostly, drowning out all attempts at conversation. Very few couples were dancing and none of them very well. The girls wore wool or cotton dresses, the boys were in flannels with jackets, shirts and ties. Her dress was pretty enough, emerald green, but it had seen better days, had felted under the arms from daily use during her last year at school and the buckle had frayed. Clothes rationing and a tight budget put paid to anything new at least until Christmas.

Suddenly a boy was standing in front of her. He was stocky, her height and wore wire-rimmed glasses. Not exactly Mr Wonderful. He was smoking a joke cigarette, twice the length of the standard brand. When he offered her one, she did not like to refuse. She thought him a little mad.

The band stopped between numbers so that conversation was possible. He had a faintly foreign accent, Hungarian, she afterwards discovered, and he had only been in Britain for four years. He was a Unitarian, which from the snobby heights of Episcopacy she thought must be some odd schismatic sect, and he had a passion for fencing. That evening he never stopped talking and cracking jokes one after the other, no doubt as nervous as she was. Although she was to see quite a lot of Hugo that first term and get to like him she was never even vaguely in love with him. It was an eye-opener to discover that you could enjoy kissing someone without being in the least in love.

She was soon to discover that finding a boyfriend was a lot easier than getting rid of one. When someone whom she found more attractive and less jokey asked her out, she was surprised by her own ability to be ruthless. Mrs C helped, of course, by saying Hugo was no longer *persona grata* in the evenings. But it was not really Hugo that Mrs C objected to. It was David. He was her first cousin, the only male cousin among a clutch of females and he was finishing his Honours English degree at Edinburgh, having started it at St Andrews. David, tall, emaciated, cadaverous and with bad teeth had a host of problems, alcoholism being only one of them, but she liked him and was intrigued by him mainly because he had published a book on Scottish Universities and was writing another about Edinburgh pubs. Betty's mother invited him to spend the Easter vacation at Shanwell because she was sorry for him. She had always thought his family had been unkind to him. His parents who lived in Malaya had left him in England with a bridge-playing, chain-smoking grandmother and his three uncles, including Betty's father, had taken no interest in the poor boy who was the sole surviving male to carry on the family name. His one wish was to visit the family home in Orkney but he was never asked. That Easter he and Betty became good friends to the extent of bickering most of the time. He chased her round the garden with a rake because she had laughed at his efforts to make a bonfire.

David had a permanent smokers' cough and whenever Betty invited him in for evening coffee Mrs C said she could not sleep for hearing him hack away in the room below. In the end she suggested Betty would be wiser to get down to her studies rather than entertain so late at night so the evening visitors were stopped. David, having got his degree that summer, left Edinburgh and she did not see or hear from him again until many years later.

She met Ben at one of Professor Gray's thrice-weekly Political Economy lectures. Felicity, who was already engaged, told her in the language of the day that 'he was dying to meet her', so it was arranged. Ben, in her mother's jargon, was a catch. An ex-naval officer, he was older than the average student, handsome in an understated way, old-fashioned in his manners, public school and a parson's son. Ben was a nice man. He too had a landlady from heaven. Sometimes she went to tea there, sometimes Mrs C invited him to tea at Beech Terrace. She liked Ben. Betty liked Ben too. She invited him back to Shanwell for a weekend and he was given the seal of approval by Uncle Bob, Aunt Nell's husband and her mother's brother, a Brigadier on leave at the time, who called him 'a sound chap'.

She made the mistake of telling Mother that she had spent VE Day with him publicly celebrating with the crowds in Princes Street Gardens, then, in the evening privately celebrating in his digs with tea and apple pie. Mother was horrified. Uncle Bob was given the dreadful task of telling her that visiting a young man's digs at night was off limits. Poor Uncle Bob. 'Not done, you know,' he managed to say several times. They both did a lot of embarrassed giggling. Once again she learned to hold her tongue.

What she did not understand about Ben was that being that much older than herself with the war behind him, he was ready to marry and settle down. When he proposed to her on a sunny spring day in a wood near Rosslyn Chapel, she could not bring herself to refuse him outright, so she prevaricated, 'maybe one day in a year or two' and promised to wear his ring - two diamonds and a sapphire - on a cord around her neck. But she knew, as she had always known that she was not in love with him, nor ever would be, for right from her third week at varsity she had already met the man she knew she would one day marry.

On Sundays there was church. That first week she had gone with the C family to the Presbyterian church at Holy Corner in

Morningside. The building was warm, plush, packed and the service interminable. The following Sunday she tried St Johns Episcopal Church in Princes Street. The church was also warm, plush, packed and the service familiarly boring. Good old Matins. You knew where you were with Matins. On the third Sunday, on the advice of her rector in Kinross who was a family friend, she finally found her way to Old St Pauls, and there she stayed.

She had got off the tram at the High Street and after a lot of time wasted in searching, finally found Carrubber's Close, a steep stone stairway that connected the High Street to Jeffrey Street behind Waverley Station. Not a prepossessing place with no hint of what lay behind the unimpressive door half-way down the Close. She knew she had come to the right place because the small plaque on the door told her that this was Old St Pauls and that she was welcome.

Tentatively she turned the handle of the door, let herself in by what happened to be the side entrance near the back - and caught her breath. Inside, three or four stone steps down, was a huge building, misty with incense and glittering with gold. It was also full of children singing a familiar hymn which might have been *Loving Shepherd of Thy Sheep*.

She wasn't listening. Her eyes were drawn to the back of the church where a young priest in a cassock was sharing a hymn-book with a couple of older children. He noticed her immediately. In that moment when their eyes met it flashed through her mind that this was the man she was going to marry.

The rest was inevitable. He left the two boys, came over to explain that the children's service was almost over and hoped she would wait for Mass? She could. The service that followed was familiar from her school days in St Andrews where she had attended All Saints, just what she liked, incense, a battalion of servers, robed boy choristers and the Scottish Liturgy performed by the elderly rector, gloriously apparelled, assisted by his two curates one of whom happened to be the priest she knew that one day she would marry. His name was Mr Marshall.

She did not see him to speak to again but next morning at Pol-Econ she told everyone she had met the man she was going to marry. Strangely enough she was in no hurry to get to know him. It would all happen, she had no doubt of that, but meanwhile there was Hugo and then Ben and then Kurt and then Charles. For the first few months it was enough to shake hands with him after the service. Then she took to going to Evensong and the handshake extended to walking back together as far as the tram stop after service. It took a whole university year to extend that walk all the way up the road to East Preston Street. He had digs not far away. By then there was no going back.

There were lunches, cinema outings and even longer walks through the Meadows until one night after Evensong during one of those walks exactly a year after her first visit to Old St Pauls, he proposed. She did not hesitate even for a moment.

Telling Mother was not so easy. In fact it was a disaster. 'She's far too young,' she told Mr Marshall, who was by now, of course, John. 'She'll never stick to you,' was Aunt Nell's comment to him. Mother was of course right. At 19, with no experience of the world or of men, Betty was indeed far too young. At 28, John could only agree. Mother made him promise that they would not see each other more than once a week for the next year. She could hardly stop Betty going to church. Betty sobbed herself to sleep that night.

They tried hard to keep the rule, John perhaps harder than Betty, but both of them knew that nothing would change. There had been an inevitability about that first glimpse of each other in church.

Cheating on her behalf took various forms. One of them involved the Old St Pauls Guide Company. The captain, S, who, with her parents and two sisters were all life-long members of the congregation, was looking for a lieutenant to help with the girls. Would she be interested? Only a couple or so years older than her, S was to become a life-long friend and Guiding was added to Betty's hectic schedule.

In her early teens, Betty had been a Guide and although she had never reached the dizzy heights of patrol leader with an armful of badges, she knew a little about Guiding. The Old St Pauls Company was fun. S was good at her job, and, although Betty was never to come to grips with the more intricate knots or the Morse code, she managed to bluff her way through. Of course her real reason for helping was the hope that Mr Marshall would look in. When he did - and he always did - the girls would collapse in giggles.

That second year with Pol-Econ safely behind her, Psychology was her main subject. This the students found so enthralling that several of the Social Science intake decided to change their course and study it seriously. Small tutorials were taught by a young German Jewish post-graduate who was studying for his doctorate. These classes of five or six tended to be held in the back rooms of pubs in a haze of cigarette smoke and beer fumes and the subject of his study was the students themselves. They listened goggle-eyed as he questioned them then analysed them. He was intensely interested in Betty's so-called 'love at first sight' experience, insisted on meeting John and then informed the whole class that John had seen Betty, dressed in her blue suit, as the Virgin Mary and she had seen him as the reincarnation of her father. She thought it all vaguely blasphemous and she certainly never told John.

In spite of the embargo, neither of them considered breaking their engagement. John bought her a ring, a solitary diamond on a thin platinum band. He made no secret of the fact that he had got it second-hand from a member of the congregation who was also a dealer (with a somewhat shady reputation) in a second-hand goods shop. On a curate's stipend, new engagement rings were out of the question. Who cared? She loved that ring and was determined to wear it openly.

There was the little matter of Ben's sapphire ring which she now knew she would have to return. That was probably one of the most painful evenings in her life. Ben was hurt and he was angry and she could only agree with him. How was it, she wondered with her fellow students, that some couples could remain friends after a break up? Ben never spoke to her again except once, months later, when they met face to face in the Overseas Club with their new partners. Both had murmured an embarrassed 'How are you?' without waiting for a reply. Ben had got together with Sylvia and Betty heard that they had subsequently married.

That second and final year of her Social Science certificate course passed in a blaze of pleasure. Studying wasn't too difficult, She always did just enough work to pass her exams but pleasure was hard work. For some reason she was in charge of organising the Social Science charity dance for Rag Week. She booked the Balmoral Ballroom in Princes Street for the venue, then realised she would also have to find a band. With only five days before the event, she was forced to visit the Caledonian Ballroom on Guide night to engage one of their five-piece bands. It took all her courage to walk through the dancers, amid their stares and the sniggers, up to the band platform wearing her Guide uniform. Fortunately they were free.

Arriving early on the evening of the dance, she realised that she had forgotten to get a license for alcohol. The Balmoral manager told her that only the Lord Provost could issue this in person at such short notice, so, with the help of her friends, she scraped together enough money for a taxi and off she sped to the Lord Provost's home recognisable by the ornate lamp post outside his house. He was more amused than annoyed at the sudden appearance of a desperate young student in her dance dress (another acquisition from John's second-hand dealer and a bit tight) on his doorstep. Then, license in hand, she returned in time to find that a contingent of Norwegian naval officers had just arrived and were looking for something stronger than fizzy lemonade.

One of them was gorgeous. As a hostess for the event, she would have liked to keep him to herself just for that evening but she had come with her best friend, a maths student called Sheila whom she had known at school and whose family were distantly related. She knew she didn't stand a chance of attracting Hans with Sheila in the room. She was probably the prettiest girl Betty had ever seen, certainly the prettiest in the ballroom and lovely with it. 'Sheila,' she said generously. 'This is Hans from Norway. Hans meet Sheila.'

It was love at first sight for them both. A couple of years later they too were married.

If Mother had been disturbed by her engagement, John's rector who was also his minder and mentor for his curacy years was equally concerned for him. Father Monie was an elderly and seemingly shy bachelor, but, having come to the ministry by way of the civil judiciary in India, appearances were deceptive. He was also shrewd and had a sense of humour. After the engagement became more or less official, he asked to see her. Finding a suitable time was difficult because Father Monie was a great deal busier than she was. Finally the arrangement was made through John for 5 pm on a Monday in the Rectory, a great cold barn of a place in Jeffrey Street, close to the main door of the church.

Her hands were damp and her heart beating faster when on the dot of five she rang the Rectory doorbell. John, having warned her that Fr Monie was a stickler for time, she had already killed some ten anxious minutes lingering in Waverley station until the big clock told her she had two minutes to go. John had also warned her that he could be a martinet, fierce with it and a despot when he needed to be, so she had no idea what to expect. She felt a little like the schoolgirl she had so lately been summoned to the housemistress's study for untidiness. Falling in love was a lot more serious than untidiness.

He came to the door in his cassock girdled with a leather belt and led her into his study where a bright fire was burning in the small black grate and an occasional table laid with tea already brewed and buttered scones. They sat down on shabby leather armchairs either side of the fire and he was unforgettably charming. He asked her about her family and she found herself talking about the death of her father which she had never done because it was still such a painful memory, her Social Study course and her friends. As she remembered it, he said very little himself but he listened. She even told him all about the 'love at first sight' experience. Afterwards she could remember no reproaches, no criticisms, not even any advice, but she left after about an hour and a half feeling that he was on her side. It was as if he had said 'You'll do,' even if he never actually used those words.

The congregation too was lovely. There were joint invitations with John to tea or supper or occasionally a concert. One of these

21

invitations was from a married ex-curate well-known for being not only a fine preacher but also a gourmet cook. Sure enough the little sausages in a creamy white sauce were different. She would never have thought of cooking sausages in a white sauce, but she had to agree that, although strange, they were good. Afterwards when she was asked if she knew what she had been eating, she had tentatively suggested sausages. They had laughed and told her 'brains'. (Although the war was over, rationing was still fierce.) She was only thankful they had not told her beforehand.

So the congregation was supportive, Father Monie had not disapproved, her mother, now that the year was up, had reluctantly yielded to the inevitable. It was high time for her to pay a visit to John's parents. His mother had helped him buy the engagement ring so he had her support, but neither she nor his father, who had recently been released from a prison camp for civilians in Shanghai, had met her, so it was time for a visit to Dumbarton.

It had been fairly obvious from the start of their relationship that she and John came from different social backgrounds. Though Mother never said it openly it was plain to see that she considered him to be 'not one of us'. Betty had been aware of this from the start but at eighteen she could not believe that it mattered. She was never to believe that it mattered and nor did John, though, from time to time he teased her mercilessly about what he called her 'middle class morality'. He considered himself to be working class when he thought about it at all. Unfortunately it mattered to his parents, though for different reasons.

Mr Marshall, senior - she never called him anything else apart from Grandad after the children arrived - had found it hard to accept his son's call to the ministry. 'No money in it,' was his main complaint. He would rather his son had made a career of his music - he had won a scholarship to a music college for his piano playing which he had declined in favour of the church and he was also a skilled organist. Mr Marshall senior cared not a jot for social backgrounds and was proud of the fact that he was 'a self-made man' who, from humble origins, had risen to be head of the Shanghai Power Company between the two wars. Imprisoned by the Japanese for the duration, he had only recently been

22

repatriated. He had made a lot of money and had invested it in Australia so most of the conversation during Betty's three days stay was about his determination to emigrate. He was disappointed, however, that John's marriage would not bring in some shekels. Betty was literally the church mouse.

Mrs Marshall - Betty never called her Jean - was reluctant to leave Dumbarton and would not even consider emigrating until after the wedding. Her main reason for not wanting to go was understandable. She had buried her second son, Matt, only a few years before in Dumbarton after he had died of heart complications from rheumatic fever. But go they eventually did, built themselves a fine bungalow in Pymble, a suburb of Sydney, stuck it for ten years and then came home. The irony was it was he who was determined to return to Scotland. She would have preferred to remain in the warmth and comfort of their fine new home. Meanwhile her only comment on the engagement had been, 'Why couldn't you have chosen a nice girl from Dumbarton?' She had even picked one out. She and Betty worked hard at their relationship.

But that was for the future. Meanwhile there were exams to sit and a wedding to plan.

Somehow those last two terms at varsity lost their significance in the light of her engagement and her involvement with the congregation. So little did they matter that when it came to graduating, she got the day wrong. She borrowed the necessary black skirt and gown. Mother and Aunt Nell came through to Edinburgh only to find that the ceremony had taken place the day before. She picked up her scroll in its imposing red cardboard tube the following day from the office. She was only mildly disappointed.

Mother too had other matters on her mind. With the war over, and when Uncle Bob, a regular soldier, had recovered from his war wound, decisions had to be taken. Shanwell was riddled with dry rot and needed to be rewired throughout for electricity so Uncle Bob made the sad decision to sell the old family home. Mother therefore had to find a new house for herself and her daughters and funds were limited.

Her first thought was St Andrews, a town she had known all her life, but both of Betty's sisters were against the idea. They were still at boarding school in that town and could not bear the thought of becoming day-girls. St Andrews was also an expensive place to live.

She looked at houses in and around Kinross but nothing seemed suitable. Then Betty's godmother, one of Mother's close friends, suggested a move north to the Black Isle where she lived. She even had a house to sell, a four-bedroom bungalow built before the war with a spectacular view across the Moray Firth, which had become vacant on the death of an old cousin. Why not come and see it?

Mother and her sisters went, liked the house and the small town, Fortrose. They moved in July 1946. It was as easy as that.

John too had a decision to make. His curacy at Old St Pauls was due to end that autumn. It had always been his ambition to enlist in the army, but when in 1939 he had tried, he had been told to go back and finish his priestly training and then he might be of some use. Thus, instead of finding a second curacy which was the practice in those days, he had offered his services to the army and been accepted as a Chaplain to the Forces, 4th class with the acting rank of captain. One of her closest friends at varsity, Barbara, was the elder daughter of the Chaplain General. According to her, he too was pleased. A date for the marriage was set to coincide with his first posting.

Reflections

There were some in the Old St Pauls congregation and amongst my friends, who said to me in all seriousness with shiny eyes. 'It was the Lord who brought you together.' Although I never denied it, I found such talk embarrassing. God was certainly a big presence in my life but far too holy, far too high and mighty to descend to marriage brokerage. I could never believe in God as the supreme draughts player who juggled his pieces around the board fixing marriages and deaths and sometimes total wipe-outs. Such beliefs I found too facile. God belittling.

So then how did I see God in those days? As an Episcopalian most certainly. My lack of class-consciousness in society did not extend to religion. Importantly I was a Scottish Episcopalian as distinguished from an Anglican. Scottish Episcopalians were in full communion with the Anglican church but we were not the same. We were not - and never had been - the 'English Church' as so many mistakenly and annoyingly still dub us. We were not some inferior outpost of Anglicanism. Far from it. We were the only province in the Anglican Communion which had not been founded by Henry VIII or English imperialism. The Episcopal Church in Scotland, just as the Presbyterian Church in Scotland, is an indigenous Reformed Church dating from 1560. John Knox was in fact an Episcopalian; he used a prayer book and he believed in bishops. Charles II recreated us as 'the Church of Scotland' and so we remained until we were perceived to support the Jacobite cause rather than the Hanoverian monarchy. For that, Episcopalians were persecuted, their churches burned and their priests imprisoned until 1789 when they agreed to pray for George III. The Anglican church did not recognise us until 1804 and there was no two-way exchange of Orders until 1864. So I was brought up to be exclusively Episcopalian and fiercesomely proud of it. I saw it as the true Church of Scotland and infinitely superior to the Church of England. Henry VIII for heavens sake!

Naively I also considered Presbyterianism and Roman Catholicism inferior to Episcopalianism. Other denominations had not yet registered. Hugo's Unitarianism sounded Jewish to me which was intriguing in an exotic way. The SEC still prayed on Good Fridays for the conversion of the Jews.

Episcopalianism came in three varieties; 'low church' which was almost on a par with Anglicanism. 'Middle of the road' was comfortably acceptable. Little St Pauls in Kinross was 'middle of the road', familiar, full of friendly faces although few in number. Anglo-Catholicism, or 'high church' was the upper crust of Episcopalianism. I was, by inheritance and inclination, 'high church'. I sank to my knees at the *Incarnatus* half way through the

25

creed and scrambled up again in good time to cross myself at the end. My father had been 'high church', the proud grandson of John Mason Neale, scholar, theologian and author, who had been responsible for some sixty hymns in the English Hymnal, a clutch of novels, some like *The Egyptian Wanderers* for children and a history of the Russian Orthodox Church for which the Tsar gave him £100. His membership of the Oxford Movement and the fact that had his health been better he would have become Provost of St Ninians Cathedral, Perth, redeemed him, in my eyes, for being born an Anglican. He had been barred by his bishop from his own altar in East Grinstead and stoned for his 'high church' practices. He had been my father's guiding star, and therefore he became ours. We sang a lot of John Mason Neale's hymns at every church I ever attended.

Of the few churches I had experienced by the time I was twenty, St Pauls Cathedral in Dundee, where my father had been Provost throughout the thirties, had basically been a Matins place. Although it had 'lights and vestments', it was determinedly 'middle of the road'. Interminable *Te Deums* only occasionally varied by the even longer *Benedicite* dominated Sunday morning worship. Sermons were endless gobbledygook. I got out of the habit of listening to sermons at an early age, and it took a long time to learn how to hear them. My father tried hard to replace Matins as the main Sunday morning service with the newly published Scottish Prayer Book liturgy and succeeded only once a month, which he saw as failure.

All Saints in St Andrews, which I had attended during my school years, was unashamedly 'high'. It smelled of wood polish and incense. Instead of pews there were chairs with rush seats, and exceedingly uncomfortable kneelers. There was no way you could slouch in what was known as the 'shampoo position'. The Scottish Liturgy was celebrated at Low Mass at 8 and High Mass with incense at 10 am. Sunday School was at 3 pm and Evensong followed by Benediction, at 6. The rector, Piers Holt Wilson, Peter to our family, was my father's best friend. He had prepared me for Confirmation and heard my first confession. He was full of fun and laughter and kindness, with a wife who was considered rather

26

'fast' because she played bridge and partied, and two sophisticated daughters who were older than me and much cleverer.

No one who considered him or herself to be a true Episcopalian received Communion at the mid-morning service. That was considered to be slightly improper and only excusable in the old and infirm. As soon as I was confirmed, I was expected to attend 'early church', as it was called, at 8 am on alternate Sundays and preferably every week. Nor did you eat or drink before receiving Communion. I found 'early church' hard. At school it meant giving up that delicious Sunday extra hour in bed and at home there was a three-mile bike ride often in the dark to get to little St Pauls.

Also as a teenager I had an alarming tendency to feel dizzy at the early service and often had to leave All Saints in a hurry and crouch on a bench in the porch while my housemistress pushed my head between my knees. After a spectacular faint at St Pauls, Kinross, one early Christmas morning when my plump teenaged body crashed across the aisle and landed at the feet of an elderly gentleman in the opposite pew - I came to, convinced he was Santa Claus - I was persuaded to have a cup of hot tea and a biscuit before the early service. I always felt this was cheating, but for me it was also a punishment. In those days I hated tea. Instead I developed methods to stop myself passing out. The moment I felt my head swim I would dig my fingernails into the soft flesh of my arm or bite the inside of my mouth until pain dominated my thoughts. I believed that if I could think myself into fainting (which my housemistress was convinced I did), I could equally think myself conscious. Mostly it worked but at a price. Early church was always a small cross.

Few St Leonards girls went to All Saints. The majority were Anglicans who attended St Andrews Church which was spectacularly 'low'. I attended St Andrews Church only once in my whole six and a half years at school and that was for my Confirmation. There again I was a complete snob. The girls who attended St Andrews were Anglicans and therefore in my opinion a lesser breed of Christian. They knew no better.

My religious snobbery extended into early married life. I once earnestly told a respectable elderly Presbyterian that she was in schism. There was an almighty row. The woman in question complained loudly to anyone who would listen that she had been insulted and there were shocked intakes of breath. John too was angry with me. It had been our first serious row.

'How could you speak to her like that?' he asked.

'Well it's true, isn't it?'

He hadn't answered directly. 'It's true that you were unkind.'

When my apology was grudgingly accepted, I was duly chastened but deep down still convinced I was right. It was many years before I started to grow up a bit in the faith.

Right from those early days at OSP I enjoyed John's services. There was just the right degree of informality, which, combined with reverence and a complete lack of arrogance, tugged at my soul. As he grew older, his right knee turned as leathery as the soles of his feet from genuflecting His sermons were deceptively simple and contained one message only. He believed that no preacher at Mass should exceed ten minutes (fifteen at Matins). If you couldn't get your message over in ten minutes then it was not worth preaching. He spent a lot of time on his sermons memorising them so that they appeared extempore but if you listened carefully there was not one wasted word. Though I still found other preachers hard to follow, I understood his instantly and I was never bored. Seeing that I had to listen to a good many of his sermons that was a great gift to me. That and the fact that with him I always felt safe in the faith. He would be good for both of us.

So, how then did I see God in those busy varsity days? Looking back on it I think the psychologist spoke a great deal of sense. Part of that instant attraction was undoubtedly the fact that John was a priest as my father had been, and, in many ways, particularly since his death, my father had been my role model for God, but my tutor did not, perhaps, see far enough. John may have been the priest my father had been certainly but he was also the priest that I would have chosen to be. Through him, and through my choice of social work, I had found some sort of vicarious vocation.

Chapter Two

Marriage

Betty should have been married in October 1946 not long after her twentieth birthday. Her sisters were to be her bridesmaids, the setting St Andrews Episcopal Church, Fortrose, the celebrant the Right Revd Piers Holt Wilson, (Peter) who had been her Rector in St Andrews, and was now the Bishop of Moray, Ross and Caithness. He had been one of her father's colleagues and a close family friend.

She was by this time living happily as a 'daughter at home' in her mother's new bungalow overlooking the Moray Firth in Fortrose and preparing for her marriage in the early autumn. One morning shortly before the wedding, John had gone down to Father Monie's study and found him dead; a shattering experience for him for he had loved his rector. Because he was needed at OSP, the marriage was postponed until December 31. The RAChD (Royal Army Chaplains' Department) gave him permission to postpone his chaplaincy for three months or until cover could be found for the parish so on a cold but bright morning on the last day of 1946 they were married at 10 am followed by a Nuptial Mass and a reception held at the Deanery generously hosted by the Rector, Edgar Dobson, and his kind wife Doris. Most of the congregation including her best friend, Sheila was there and her sisters were both bridesmaids. The champagne ran out before she herself could have a glass but the cake made by her godmother was delicious. All too soon it was time to catch the afternoon train to Edinburgh. After a two-night stay in the Cockburn Hotel in Edinburgh where John, in his clerical collar, had the small embarrassment of having to present his ration book along with hers still in her maiden name, they started married life in the rectory in Jeffrey Street.

Nevertheless they managed two snatched midweek honeymoons; one to Gullane for two nights in appalling January weather and the other the following week in a vast empty hydro in Dunoon where they spent most of the time playing table tennis in equally appalling weather. The week after that, John had to report to the War Office so she went too and they spent two nights in an annex of the Gloucester Hotel in Baker Street.

That was the winter of the chilblains. In London she could hardly walk for the pain in her feet. Her clothes ration had long ago gone so they tried three shoe shops before they found one which would accept John's army coupons in exchange for a pair of fur lined boots and a substantial dollop of wedding present money. Joy; she could walk again. (Whatever happened to chilblains? They used to be an annual occurrence causing itchy agonising swellings on the toes and fingers. Now, like frosted windows and iced-over tooth mugs, they seem to have gone, thank God.) With the boots snug on her feet, they managed to cram in visits to the Tower, Madame Tussaud's, a theatre and a film.

Back at the rectory she attempted her first bash at hospitality by giving a lunch party, a very small lunch party. The congregation at OSP had consisted of every age and every class. Among the older members, Miss Stag, an energetic spinster, had been unfailingly kind and supportive. Tiny, elderly and lame, she organised the choristers, ran the Child Garden and the clergy with consistent good humour. She had taken John and Betty to her heart providing meals, concert tickets and gentle advice. (Most congregations have their Miss Stags, she was eventually to discover.) So Miss Stag was to be their first invited guest.

The menu would consist of John's (and Betty's) favourite food, steak and kidney pie and steamed treacle pudding and custard. The rectory kitchen was well supplied with cooking pots and pudding basins. Unfortunately they were all enormous. The recipes which she found in an old book in one of the kitchen drawers were for large numbers thus the ensuing steak and kidney pie was of massive proportions while the steamed pudding made properly with black treacle could have fed the whole congregation. Tiny Miss Stag struggled manfully with the first course but when the steamed pudding appeared she wilted. Both John and Betty, however, had no such difficulty.

Army life properly started a month later in Lochmaben. John was on a six months posting to an officers' training depot in the

Borders. As there were no army quarters, nor would she have qualified for one if there had been, they both stayed as permanent residents in the local family-owned hotel where the price was reduced in exchange for her help in the kitchen. In charge of the soup pot which she kept topped up daily with vegetables and meat bones, she also hefted the hoover along endless passages and gossiped with the staff. When John had time off they rowed on Lochmaben or walked around its shores. Not for long however. A visit to the local doctor confirmed she was pregnant so in April she paid her first visit home.

In 1947 the best means of transport from Inverness to Fortrose was by train. It was a long tedious journey first from Dumfries to Edinburgh, then on to Inverness where her mother met her. They caught the north train and then changed to the Black Isle branch line at Muir of Ord. The small local engine chugged through innumerable little stations and finally arrived half an hour later at Fortrose. It was on that train that she broke the news of her pregnancy to her mother. To her amusement and chagrin she saw her mother counting off the months on her fingers. It was considered good form in those days to wait at least six months before conceiving. With Betty it had been about two weeks.

She had no time to enjoy the holiday. That night she developed a pain. Dr Anderson diagnosed appendicitis so she was taken by ambulance into hospital and operated on the next day.

It was while she was recuperating at home that John received his first proper posting, three years in Kenya, a gift of a job which her university friend Bar's father, the Chaplain General, believed they would both enjoy. Unfortunately army rules dictated that she could not travel after she was six months pregnant or before the baby was six months old. It was decided, therefore, that she would stay with her mother, have the baby at home and travel out as soon as it could be arranged thereafter.

Seeing John off after his embarkation leave was almost more than she could bear. They arranged to go to the cinema, a few yards from the station in Inverness. He would slip away at the appropriate time so she could weep her usual buckets in the dark. Two days later he rang. The boat train to Liverpool had crashed.

He was unhurt but his embarkation was postponed until another passage could be arranged. In fact he had had a crushing experience when the train crashed. Unhurt himself, he found his way to the injured but when he had offered to pray with a man who had been badly hurt he had been told in no uncertain terms to 'bugger off'. That had upset him. He had returned to Fortrose where he and Betty had to go through the whole agonising performance in the cinema all over again a fortnight later. She never got used to saying goodbye.

That year at home in Fortrose was filled with happiness. The fact that her mother as yet had no car and no telephone were only minor inconveniences. Her godmother was generous with both. John's letters came regularly, she kept well and 1947 was a brilliant summer. The community was, as most communities were in those days, friendly and welcoming with a lively sprinkling of eccentrics. Church members and Auntie Sine's friends showered them with invitations to tea parties. Her mother acquired Jessie Jean from the neighbouring village of Avoch to help with the housework and she immediately became a lynch pin, a news bulletin and a confidante. The garden was dug over and cared for by Mr Bain, who lived in Fortrose and whose sister took care of her godmother. Mr Bain planted a sweet briar hedge around the garden, strawberries and raspberries and a variety of vegetables while mother took care of the flowers. Betty and any one else willing to help weeded or pulled Stinking Willie (ragwort) out of the small field that separated the house from the shore so that the local farmer could lease it for sheep or cattle.

First thing in the morning, wet or fine, Betty collected the milk in a can from Miss Bremner's brother's farm several fields away overlooking the golf course. Miss Bremner had been a lady's maid. She always wore a rusty long black dress and had a cut-glass accent. When she died they found two hundred golf balls stashed away inside the cottage.

Then she did the shopping, bicycling up the Greengates, not much more than a track in those days. The High Street was a veritable mall with Burt Miller, the butcher at the corner opposite the Bank of Scotland, who handled their meat ration. Mother always insisted he never hung his meat long enough for it was usually tough, Then the paper shop/post office which was run by Dorothy Kate, now Mrs Hayter, who had married a Canadian lumberjack recruited to work in the Black Isle forestry during the war and who now ran the local taxi service. Next to it, the Co-op, a much smaller business in those days, sold most things. On the corner opposite the Royal Station Hotel, Isa Ross's cavern of a drapery was an imposing building up a flight of stone steps. She was a small terrifying woman who refused to sell anything to you unless she approved of you. Her shop had everything from pink directoire knickers to kirbygrips and knitting wool. Everybody who was anybody patronised Miss Ross, but it was her patronage of you that mattered. Mrs Fletcher's chauffeur-driven Rolls was often to be seen drawn up outside her door while the legendary millionairess of Rosehaugh bought knitting wool and enjoyed the genteel craic. Indeed each shop every morning collected a small social gathering. Nobody just shopped. Beyond the rather grand Royal Station Hotel was Pagliari's ice-cream parlour. Had it already branched out into fish and chips? If so, she had not yet sampled his wares, but the ice cream was to die for.

On the other side of the road was Mr Stuart's licensed grocery which held the family ration books. Mr Stuart or his assistant sliced the bacon, dissected the cheeses, hacked off slabs of butter, ground coffee beans or weighed out biscuits into a paper bag, half-price if they were broken. Sometimes shoppers queued for half an hour to be served but no one seemed to mind. There was always plenty to gossip about. Below that, Mr Brooks the local electrician, sold light bulbs and batteries and lamps. Next door on the corner of Station Road was Mr Gow, the Chemist, later to be taken over by his son, Angus. Apart from prescriptions, Mr and Mrs Gow sold cosmetics and other fancy goods. Then Alexander's Bakery; Mr Alexander's toffee cakes were to die for and Mrs Alexander knew not only every customer by name but also those of their extended families. She made everyone feel instantly at home. Below her was the Tavern, said to be a rather rowdy public house which she had never entered. Rumour had it that there was still sawdust on the floor. Below that, a green grocer called Mackeddie

33

sold most things and then, opposite Burtie Butcher, the Bank of Scotland, with its imposing high counter and friendly tellers. The manager lived in a spacious flat above the bank and was a figure of enormous importance in the community.

After shopping, which took up a good deal of time most mornings, there was her godmother to visit. Sine (pronounced Sheena and Gaelic for Jean) Stuart lived with a friend Phyllis Stokes in the oldest inhabited house in Fortrose, which she had inherited from her parents and was known as Angel Court. She had hoped that Betty's mother would take over half the house which was too big for her, but Sine, in spite of her kindness and efficiency, had a strong personality and her mother was rightly afraid of her life being completely taken over by her friend. The half-mile distance between the two houses meant that her mother could keep her independence and yet enjoy the fruits of a loyal and unfailing friendship.

Sine went ahead with her decision to separate the house, retaining one half which she called Rose Court and selling the other which had the old stone angel over the porch. Her only proviso was that the buyers were Roman Catholic. From being a devout Episcopalian, Sine had converted to Catholicism and there is no one more ardent than a convert. She would annoy Mother intensely by insisting that Betty's father, had he lived longer, would have 'seen the light'. She annoyed her even more when she sat all the way through Betty's wedding, having first received permission from the local priest to attend, provided she did not take part in the worship.

Nevertheless their friendship survived such small crises and 'Auntie Sine', as Betty called her, was to remain a loving and supportive godmother till the end of her life. She introduced them to all her local friends and soon, her mother, who knew so well how to make and keep friends, had made new ones for herself. Auntie Sine also introduced her to the SWRI (Scottish Women's Rural Institute), sister organisation to the English WI, which she chaired at the time. Sine was a wonderful baker, craftswoman, gardener and organiser. Her mother's skill lay in her ability to like people for themselves so that they instinctively liked her.

34

Nevertheless she entered one of Sine's WRI baking competitions not just out of loyalty but because she believed she knew how to make pancakes. Her mother's introduction to cooking had been during the war when there was no one else to do it. Mother's selection, multi-shaped and multi-coloured from pale yellow to suspiciously dark toast-brown were duly arranged on a plate and displayed for the judges alongside plate after plate of round, plump, perfect, golden discs.

'I would na have had the nerve to put in the likes o' them,' one member remarked pointing to her mother's entry.

'Oh, nor would I,' Mother agreed earnestly. The entries were fortunately anonymous.

Afternoons were for walks and tea parties, and, in summer, picnics. Barely a day went by without a walk to the Point, about a mile, along the shore at the edge of the golf course to the Chanonry Lighthouse. Three wooden piers, evenly spaced between the Lighthouse and the harbour poked out across the stony shingle into the sea, left over from war-time when the Black Isle was a restricted zone and the D Day landings rehearsed.

One of the most unpleasant tasks her mother ever asked her to do was to drown a litter of new-born kittens by dropping them in a weighted sack over the end of one of those piers. In those days it was a regular and necessary occurrence for poor Mother who loved all animals (even Horrible, the stray tom that haunted the garden). Over the years, the piers gradually disintegrated and finally disappeared. For Betty they were always associated with that unforgettable little act of murder.

But the golf course had other delights. Besides the wild flowers, the porpoises (no dolphins that she knew of in those days), the skylarks and spectacular views across the Firth, there were mushrooms. They grew in random profusion on the greens and in the rough. The myth was that they sprang up overnight and you had to pick them first thing in the morning before the maggots got them and before Miss M, bicycling with her dog from Fortrose - mushroom-finder in chief - got there first. There was also a very cross old gentleman who lived in a hut at the far end of the golf course who waved his stick and swore at them for stealing 'his' mushrooms. Usually there were enough for all. This was before the days of chemical fertilisers. Years later poor Miss M landed up in hospital with severe food poisoning from eating golf course mushrooms.

Betty walked there most afternoons just as she dipped into the sea most mornings before breakfast in the old black wool bathing suit that had been her mother's and which stretched obligingly and indecently to contain her bump.   Her head was full of dreams about the baby she was carrying, hoping against hope that it might be a boy because she had never had a brother. Girls dominated in her generation with only one male out of eight female cousins. She did not really believe a boy was possible so she kept her hopes to herself.

Tea parties were the most popular form of entertainment in those early post-war years.   They started at 4 pm and you never left earlier (and only sometimes later) than 5 30. Those were the unspoken rules. The food consisted of tiny sandwiches, scones or pancakes with butter-pats and homemade jam, and at least two kinds of cake and shortbread. Sometimes it was just Betty and Mother invited but mostly these were parties where you met people 'of ones own sort' as the expression was. Manners were important and you usually changed into a better coat and skirt or a cleaner cotton dress.

There were dances too, reel parties for the teenagers home from boarding school in the holidays and Northern Meeting balls all of which Betty missed out on that first winter but which her sisters thoroughly enjoyed.

Much of the social life revolved around St Andrews church. The rector was a small, dark, arthritic man with a fiercely witty tongue that could at times be cruel. He had a habit of castigating from the pulpit the small, somewhat resentful congregation present for the non-attendance of absentees. He also preached against the evils of lipstick when she was the only person in the church wearing it. After she had got over her indignation and thought about it she realised it made sense.   She had no right to wear lipstick when receiving from the communal cup.   In those days it was considered sacrilege to wipe the chalice between communicants. No one, it was believed, caught germs from such a sacred source. Besides wine was a disinfectant, wasn't it? That was to change almost overnight with the coming of AIDS.

She was always a little afraid of Canon Dobson but respected him as a priest. His family she loved, especially ten-year old little Robert who would visit her and play endless games of cards with her to their mutual enjoyment. Mrs Dobson was generally and rightly considered to be a saint. She played the organ adequately when there was no-one else, organised and held the weekly women's Work Party in the Deanery, took over the SWRI when Auntie Sine moved away, baked incessantly, befriended the old, the ill-tempered and the lonely. All was done without arrogance and fuss and not always with the full support of her quick-tempered husband. Many put up with his little squalls for her sake.

There were two doctors in Fortrose at that time, Dr John Anderson and a newcomer, Dr Jack Anderson (no relation), recently demobbed from the Navy. Dr John was a remote and powerful figure, Provost of the Burgh, a taciturn man but a highly respected practitioner. Dr Jack was friendly, easy-going and his wife, Jean, had had a son born a month before Michael. Once a week Betty packed his pram with spare nappies and pushed it to the neighbouring village of Rosemarkie where the Andersons lived in a cottage overlooking the shore. They would spend the afternoon together and often the evening too, gossiping, and admiring each other's babies. Secretly she thought her own infinitely superior. Michael was long and lean and wiry, Hugh, pink and placid and rather plump.

Michael had been Dr Jack's first baby after his war years in the Navy, and, according to her midwife, more nervous and clumsy than any student. She was past noticing. The private midwife or 'monthly nurse', as she was called, came a week before the baby was due and stayed for three weeks afterwards. Both Betty and Mother were deeply in awe of her and also profoundly grateful. Although she spent the long hours of labour regaling Betty with horrific birth stories, she could not have been more efficient. She did everything for Betty and the baby so that all Mother had to do was cook. She also got Michael into a routine: feeds at 6 and 10 am. 2, 6 and 10 pm. Tea-time was playtime when he lay and kicked on the heath-rug before a well-guarded fire. Bath time followed at about 5 pm to which neighbours who had come for tea were invited to watch. At four days old, he was outside in his pram every morning behind a cat net, provided the weather did not blow a gale, and he was taken for a walk every afternoon. What happened if he woke and cried in the night she never knew for he slept next door in the nurse's room and Betty had previously expressed milk so that she did not need to be disturbed. He was well trained and so, indeed, was she. When her other children arrived, she was always to be grateful for what she had learned from Nurse Fraser.

A new baby was an event in Fortrose's fairly top-heavy community of friends and neighbours. Those six months of winter were a delight with Kenya to look forward to in April 1948 when her passage on the SS SCYTHIA came through.

Mother accompanied her on a nightmarish journey in an over-crowded train to Liverpool where they stayed in the Adelphi Hotel for a night and a taxi took her and Michael to the dock early the following morning.

Reflections

Half way through my marriage ceremony I began to cry. All through the signing of the register in the vestry, I cried. These were not tears of sorrow. Far from it. Nor had they much to do with joy, though I was aware of being happy. They had to do with religion. My father had cried at the drop of a hat. He had wept in the pulpit while preaching his last sermon in St Pauls Cathedral and I had been embarrassed for him. I was acutely embarrassed when my tears, entirely unbidden and unwanted, started to flow as Bishop Peter pronounced John and me man and wife, nor did they stop until the Nuptial Mass was over. They were connected in some way to God, goodness and nobility (the royal family for instance and the National Anthem still occasionally bring tears). They also had lot to do with the loss of my father certainly and even more to do with saying goodbye, but they were also, I believe, inherited. The tear gene I considered to be a family curse.

Somebody in the vestry where we signed the register had a handkerchief which I clung on to till the end of the service. I was fine during the reception in the Deanery, waved goodbye quite cheerfully as Ted Hayter's taxi took us to Inverness Station, but then on the train John said, 'Your mother looked so sad when you said goodbye', and that finished me. In spite of the fact that the train was crowded with raucous people going home for New Year's Eve celebrations, the tears started and would not stop. It was like saying goodbye on the way back to boarding school, but this time it was forever.

I was very devout during that first year of marriage, attending all three services for the short period we stayed in the rectory in OSP and then in Fortrose, every Sunday, making my confession and regularly visiting the older and less able members of the congregation. One of these Fortrose members - ancient, confused and contentious - known locally as Bo-Peep because of her cape and the crook she invariably carried, or 'the Little Wayside Flower' because her name was Violet, lived in a shockingly run-down cottage in Academy Street. I was the only person she allowed over the threshold to help her fill in the holes in her ancient clay and wattle walls with a paste made of flour and water. She was very afraid of thieves and understandably so. Her tumble-down little home was full of priceless pictures and ornaments.

Then there were 'Dranners and Manners', two elderly sisters, the former of whom had been the last parson of Arpafeelie's wife, who thrived on gossip and bridge and was the rector of Fortrose's scourge. Jeanie V, in her forties who had been starved of oxygen as an infant and thus had never properly grown up, used to come with me on picnics to Rosemarkie beach or by train to concerts given by popular singers like Robert Wilson in Inverness or for walks up Fortrose Hill. I let her down badly over my wedding. Jean adored new clothes. Her dragon-lady of a mother had told her to ask me what I would like her to wear for the occasion. She desperately needed me to say 'a new outfit', but I wasn't thinking. I told her I liked her old pink tweed suit so her mother told her to wear it. Jean's other passion was presents, not for herself but for giving as birthday and Christmas gifts. She haunted every church or village sale with her few shillings pocket-money which would all go on 'suitable' gifts. I still have her carefully chosen coat-hangers. But God was Jean's first and foremost love. She never missed a service and if you sat in front of her in church, as I did, you could hear her touching murmured little prayers.

I suppose it was all good practice for the years of parish life that lay ahead but the truth was I enjoyed visiting. When Michael was born I wheeled him from one friend to another, basked in their praise of the baby and enjoyed their tea and conversation. Yes, looking back on it, I would have particularly enjoyed that part of a priest's life and no doubt grown somewhat fat, like so many priests on too many cakes and cups of tea.

And God? Remote, stern, good to you if you said your prayers (dutifully on your knees by your bed night and morning) attended services and read your passage from the Bible Reading Fellowship booklet. True he expected a lot from you, but that was because he had already given you so much in the first place. Mr Be-done-by-as-you-did.

Canon Dobson was my first visitor after Michael was born. He stood at the door and blessed us both and then took out his diary and arranged with me when I should be 'churched', as it was called in those days. The service is still there in the Scottish Prayer Book immediately after the *Public Baptism of Such as are of Riper Years* and it's called *The Thanksgiving of Women after Child-Birth: Commonly called The Churching of Women.* It's a beautiful short act of praise and thanksgiving, and, though at the time I was far too nervous fully to appreciate the words, yet in my heart I could not have been more grateful for my gift of a son. Michael was baptised when he was a month old with Canon Dobson as the only Godparent able to be present. Most of the congregation came to the service and Auntie Sine made a splendid Christening cake.

Yes, had I been asked, I would have said that God was a fatherly task-master, but mostly I took him for granted. My yoke was easy and my burden light.

Chapter Three

Africa

SS SCYTHIA had been a luxurious cruise ship before the war and was now converted into a troop ship with the officers and an assorted bunch of wives and children on the top decks and the other ranks segregated below. Betty's cabin, once a first class apartment, now resembled the black hole of Calcutta crammed with eighteen berths for women and children. Michael was the youngest passenger so she had been allotted a lower berth with a deep string cradle slung over her rail. She also had one of only two portholes available. Like herself, the other wives expected no better.

For the first three days she was wretchedly seasick. Her new companions, those that were still upright and most of them seasoned army wives, rallied round with their pet remedies all of which contained generous measures of brandy. The result was that Michael, who was not yet fully weaned, was happy. He stood up in his string cot swinging himself contentedly and laughing at whoever was kind enough to notice him.

After three days she acquired her sea legs and began to enjoy herself.

There was much to enjoy. Dancing, a lot of dancing, Tombola or Housey-Housey (as Bingo was then called), deck quoits, sunbathing in canvas chairs, and wonderful food, or so it seemed after the rigours of British rationing. Several wives remained in the cabin to baby-sit each evening thus allowing the others to take part in whatever had been planned in the Officers Mess. Sometimes they got into trouble.

One morning half way through the voyage the other padre's wife on board who was in the adjacent eighteen-berth cabin, came to her in great distress. She and the three other women baby-sitting the previous evening had been reported to the O.C. Troops for gambling in the cabin. They had been playing Shove-ha'penny for guess what? - ha'pennies. Poor Mrs G. She was sure that the disgrace would blight her husband's career. He had been a chaplain all through the war, was to be John's superior officer in the Chaplain's department in East Africa and was looking for further promotion. It had never occurred to Betty that she herself might have blighted John's career. She too had been reported to the O.C Troops for a much more serious crime.

Fresh water was strictly rationed on a ship that held many hundreds of soldiers. All clothes and bodies had to be washed in salt water. Michael was the only child in nappies on the ship. Salt water gave him a rash, so early one morning, she sneaked into the bathroom and washed out two nappies in fresh (albeit cold) water. Of course she was seen and reported. The O.C. Troops sat at a desk in his small office with the adjutant behind him, and reminded her of Uncle Bob. He too was a brigadier and had been embarrassed. 'Not done, you know. Bit selfish. Shortage of fresh water. Understand why...' etc. She wanted to explain, make excuses, giggle a bit, but in fact she left the room without uttering a single word except to mumble shamefacedly that she was sorry. Later that day the O.C.Troops wife, Lady someone or other, who was mostly invisible, sent her a jar of zinc and castor oil ointment which helped with the nappy rash. It had never occurred to her that John's career might be blighted.

Housey-Housey was a new game to her. (Later, under the name of Bingo, it was to become a regular feature of parish fund-raising.) In the lounge used as the Officer's Mess which was disproportionately full of raucous young National Servicemen, it became a riot. Suddenly someone was thrusting up her card and shouting 'House!' She had won about five pounds which in 1948 was a considerable sum of money. Having been told by the same young man (naively, she believed him) that it had to be spent on drinks all round, she found herself by the end of the evening the poorer by a few pence. The same happened with the game of Liar Dice. It turned out to be only vaguely connected with the game of the same name she had played with the family at home. This time she was decidedly the poorer by more than a few pence.

The women passengers had been warned by the O.C Troops in a pep talk she had missed because of her seasickness (but of which she was immediately informed) that shipboard romances were to

42

be avoided. Young soldiers were all too easily aroused when the sun shone and there was little else to do. It was up to the women to control the situation by refusing to go up to the boat deck at night. Forewarned was to be fore-armed. The proof of this she was somewhat shockingly to discover for herself.

Among the mass of soldiery, a handful of civilian men had been allotted passages. One of these she got to know, yes, and on the boat deck. It was her custom to get up early and take Michael, who was always awake at about five, up to the top deck before the first sitting for breakfast to crawl about in the sun before it got too hot. Apart from a few health fanatics doing press-ups or skipping there were very few other early risers apart from Steven. He was a thin, sad, young man dressed in dark trousers and a white shirt who was always on his own. Civilians on a troop ship were considered to be a lesser breed when they were thought about at all. Watching Michael, they became friends. She was quickly sorry for him for it was soon obvious that he was not only desperately homesick but also lonely. Young though he was, he had a wife and family of two little boys at home in Britain. They had decided to emigrate to Kenya where he had some sort of job waiting for him in the colonial service, and he had gone out ahead of his family to find them a new home.

Soon it became a regular event, that morning tryst, when he would pour out his heart to her, while, she, to her shame, only half listened, being far more interested in Michael's efforts to stand and the sparkling sun and sea. Listening to Steven for an hour before breakfast was tolerable but soon he began to interrupt her at other times of the day when she was gossiping with her new women friends or learning chess from a couple of friendly National Servicemen or having a drink in the bar with her cabin mates. Why wouldn't he? He thought they were friends. People noticed and commented. Today it's called stalking. She was not nice to him. Not that she actually said anything. It was more the cold shoulder while her friends raised eyebrows and huffed and puffed on her behalf. Then there were the recriminations, so, for a couple of mornings, she stopped going up to the boat deck before breakfast. When she went back there was no sign of him. In fact there was no sign of him anywhere. She was concerned enough to ask one of his cabin mates, an older major who had taken part in the Nurenburg Trials. He was very short with her. 'He's in the hospital wing,' he told her coldly. 'What happened?' she asked concerned but he turned on his heel and she realised that he was too angry to speak. Later when he had calmed down he told her he had found Steven in the shower unit having attempted to cut his wrists. 'Did you not see what was happening?' he asked her curiously. 'Could you not tell that you had turned his world upside down?'

She shook her head ashamed. She had had no idea. It was a salutary lesson of what could happen on board ship. As they entered warmer waters, she realised that several of her new friends were enjoying steamy top deck romances with certain overheated officers.

John and the other husbands whose wives were travelling were allowed on board at Mombasa. He and Michael were a little shy of each other to begin with but that soon wore off. They climbed into the back of a three-ton army vehicle and were whisked off to the Army Transit Camp at Nyali Beach to await transport to John's depot, 303 (East Africa) Training and Depot Regiment in Nanyuki, several hundreds of miles up country.

The camp at Nyali was everyone's dream holiday destination. Warm blue seas, golden sands, miles and miles of them, and just above the dunes a dozen or so not uncomfortable Nissen huts built under tall palm trees and surrounding an imposing building - the officer's mess - where army families or single officers on leave or in transit relaxed in the bar ('rum and coco-cola' as quoted in the pop song, was the tipple of the day), dined in a first class restaurant and danced in a large airy lounge. It all seemed to Betty after the austerity of post-war Britain like incredible luxury.

Each family was allotted one or possibly two adjacent rooms in a hut containing four rooms. These buildings had thatched roofs and the current myth was that they harboured snakes. The only wild life she saw at that time was ants. Having left one of Michael's half-chewed Farley's rusks on her dressing table to go up to the mess dining room for a meal, she came back to find an trail of ants leading to it from under the door and another trail leaving. The

44

African servant, immaculate in white kanzu and wide blue cummerbund, laughed and showed her how to store foodstuffs on a dish in her wash basin filled with water.

Two days later they took the evening train, a night and two days' journey up country to Nanyuki, a small township in the foothills of Mount Kenya. The train, entirely run by Indians, consisted of individual compartments with no connecting corridor, one per family, where the seats folded down into sleeping berths and with an *en suite* wash-basin and lavatory. To have a meal, passengers had to leave the train at a convenient station, walk down the platform and climb up into the restaurant car, eat, wait for the next station and clamber out again. All safe and easy as the train waited for at least fifteen minutes at every station. So, after a good meal, the train stopped, they got off, but, horror of horrors, this was not a station. They were out on the track in the pitch-black night and the train had begun to move on. Hastily John thrust open the first compartment door to hand. A very surprised colonel and his wife were forced to admit them. There followed an awkward few minutes which seemed like hours to Betty, who was aware that Michael's nappy needed changing. The colonel's wife, an awesomely smart American, did her best to laugh it off and fortunately the proper station was only about ten minutes on. They were not to make that mistake again. After a good night's sleep, they dared to leave the train at Nairobi to wolf down a substantial breakfast of bacon and eggs and get back into their own compartment before the train moved off.

After Nairobi the train began to climb so slowly that she was able to open the compartment door and sit with her feet on the high running step and watch Africa go by. Everywhere there were little black totos running alongside them, laughing, offering bananas for a few pence, men and women in colourful clothes who stopped whatever they were doing to wave. Already she loved Africa.

There were two hotels in Nanyuki both well patronised by the British farming settlers and the Army and both fierce rivals. The myth was that one was run by a British Israelite and the other by Jehovah's Witnesses. The latter received guidance to close the bar thus sending all their customers winging across the township to the other. They were soon to receive guidance to re-open the bar with free drinks all round. The other, the Outspan, where she was to stay for about a week before their accommodation was finalised, had a painted line marking the Equator running right through the bar.

Her first purchase in one of the well-stocked Indian-run shops was a tin of peaches and a can of condensed milk. She had not tasted either since the start of the war, nearly nine years before. She sat in the sun and with Michael's help, glugged all the peaches and half the condensed milk. They tasted like nectar. Her first Swahili words (*Ulete magi ya moto, pesi pesi*) 'Please bring hot water quickly' to make up Michael's Farex, (a bland sort of porridge) were burned on her brain forever.

At 6000 ft, Nanyuki had an ideal climate, hot dry days, cold nights lit up with stars and amazing lightning displays. Behind them, Mount Kenya, that great Kikuyu God, showed his snow-capped peak occasionally at dawn or dusk, but most of the time he was shrouded in cloud. Only a few years earlier two Italian POWs had escaped from a British prison camp in Nanyuki to climb the mountain, their only guide being a sketch on a Bovril jar. When they had achieved this small miracle they 'escaped' back into the POW camp. Before and below them lay the plains, acres and acres of umbrella thorns and acacias shimmering in the heat. It was a beautiful place.

Not yet eligible for an army quarter, John had found private accommodation a mile or so out of the township. It consisted of three rondavel huts with mud walls and thatched roofs connected to each other by a verandah: upmarket rondavels, though, for they had parquet flooring and large comfortable fireplaces. They were the guest accommodation belonging to a neighbouring Scottish settler who lived on the other side of a paddock. She had recently been widowed and needed the money.

This then was their first home. Two African servants, a cook and a house man, lived in a hut behind the rondavels with a tiny kitchen and a charcoal stove where the cook produced excellent three-course dinners and baked rather good bread. There was a bath which only worked when the fire was lit under an oil drum at the back of the house, and ran out into a small open pond. She came out of hospital after one of her worse bouts of tonsillitis to find the bath full of soapy water and dirty nappies, three lit cigarettes fixed at various points in the bathroom and the gramophone at its loudest while John, puffing away at a fourth fag, did his best to cope with the washing. The loo was an outdoor privy with a fearsome drop.

Thuko, the house servant, did the marketing, the housework, the washing (apart from her clothes and Michael's nappies) and served the meals. Thuko was kind, excellent with Michael (*bwana kidogo*) and always good-tempered. The settlers, including her landlady, moaned about the influx of army families who ruined the Africans by over-paying them, but, to Betty, it seemed that they worked for peanuts. Thuko became a friend, or so she thought. Three years later after she had returned to Scotland she had a letter from him, obviously written by an official letter-writer for it was full of flowery phrases and exaggerated sentiments, asking if he could come to Britain to work for her there. She wished.

She had a couple of small adventures with Thuko. One morning she had crossed the field to have coffee with their landlady. Impossible to wheel the pushchair over the bumpy grass so Thuko had offered to carry Michael across. As John said, it gave him a good excuse to have a gossip with Mrs R's house servants, but in fact there was another reason. He carried a stout stick in his other hand. As they walked back, she carrying a girning Michael, Thuko - a little behind her - suddenly shoved her sideways hard in the back. She was prepared to be indignant until she saw the fat greyish green snake slither across the path exactly where she would have trodden. Thuko with his stick beat the creature savagely to death.

Later he told her that green mambas were known to inhabit that field and had already killed one of Mrs R's horses. They were deadly not only because of their poison but also because of their sluggishness. She was duly grateful.

The second time he came to her rescue the laugh was on her. Once a week John visited a neighbouring army camp at Nyeri which entailed a night away from home. She was sitting by the fire in the first of the three rondavels reading an Agatha Christie novel when she looked up to see the most enormous spider crawling down the white-washed wall close to the door on the other side of the room. Horrified, she threw her book at it and screamed. Of course the book missed as did the half-dozen others she pulled from the bookcase beside her chair. Meanwhile the beastly thing got nearer the floor. Soon it would start scuttering across the shiny wooden floor and - she screamed again and again. Within seconds Thuko and the cook flung open the door. 'What's wrong, Memsahib?' they both asked. She pointed shakily to the spider that still clung to the wall. Both of them collapsed in laughter before reassuring her that it was harmless, a kitchen spider. Thuko casually removed it in both hands and took it outside. All next day every time she saw either of the men, they collapsed in laughter which did nothing to cure her spider phobia.

Thuko had to come to her rescue yet again. This time it was 'jiggers'. These were nasty little insects that burrowed under the toenail to lay their eggs. She was told that the Africans knew exactly how to remove them with a needle. When she discovered that she had one, Thuko pricked and squeezed in the right place and out it popped.

Ticks were another problem, not with humans but with dogs.

Thieving was fairly common and as 1948 heralded the early days of Mau Mau, (Kenyan freedom fighters) everyone in the army acquired a dog for protection. When the owner was posted home, he handed it on to another incoming family. That was how they got Oor Wullie.

Useless as a guard dog, Oor Wullie was gentle, timid and incredibly scruffy. He was also infested with ticks. She would sit for hours with a cigarette tin full of paraffin and a pair of tweezers to remove them, but, by next day, they were as bad as ever. The problem was solved by one of their civilian friends, a Scottish farmer, who brought her a tin of Gamatox, which he used for his sheep. The powder worked instantly and Oor Wullie lost a lot of his scruffiness though he was never much use as a guard dog. Within a few weeks they had been robbed of all the contents of the dining-room. The military police explained that the thieves greased a toto who was small enough to climb in the window. They also took a plate of rather nasty and very stale cakes which Betty had hidden in a drawer so as not to offend the cook. With Mrs R's consent, the army fixed heavy iron stanchions across the windows to prevent further similar robberies.

John also was persuaded to acquire a gun. It was a terrifying thing which neither of them knew how to use. John decided to practise one evening and Mrs R on her verandah across the field swore the bullet whizzed by her head. He never tried again but Betty was induced to sleep with it by her pillow when he was on his weekly trip to Nyeri. Thankfully it remained unused.

Then there were the millipedes; great black creatures with hundreds of orange legs nicknamed 'Mombasa Trains'. Michael was fascinated by them and would play with them endlessly when he got the chance. On one occasion she was sitting in a deck chair with some friends while the children played in an improvised sandpit. She reached down for the cigarette tin to hand it round, opened it and to her horror found an exceptionally large Mombasa Train. Michael, about eighteen months at the time, screeched with laughter.

An encounter with a rhino was less funny. They were returning from a party at a nearby settler's farm in John's allotted transport, a fifteen-hundredweight truck plus driver. She and Michael were sitting in the back when to her horror she saw that they were being chased down the red dirt road by an enormous black rhino and it was gaining on them. The driver stepped on the accelerator, and, scared stiff, she clung on to Michael with one hand and the side of the truck with the other as they bounced over the deep ruts in the track. Fortunately the rhino lost interest, stopped and disappeared into the bushes at the side of the road.

Social life included mess functions and private parties. This was the Kenya of recent scandals and the current phrases were, 'Are you married or do you live in Kenya?' and 'Who's Whos?' Gossip was rife. Not that she ever witnessed any salacious incidences. Unpleasant yes, like the time a drunk lieutenant, at a children's party, put his lighted cigarette to Michael's balloon and scared the life out of him. Or when, at a sun-downer at a neighbouring settler's farm, she asked for orange juice, thought she had been given it, so allowed Michael to drink it only to find that half of it was gin. That involved a dash in the fifteen-hundredweight truck to the hospital where the doctor on duty, to her fury, found it all rather amusing.

Mess life included the usual dances and parties where most of the officers and not a few of their wives got mildly drunk, and horror of horrors, mixed hockey matches. Being the youngest wife in the Mess she had been included in the women's team. She had never cared for hockey at school but at least she knew the rules. Here there was no rules or so it seemed and no neat protective pads or spiked gloves. It was out and out war where the men got rougher as the game proceeded. In the end the women retreated to the sidelines and just watched in amazement as the men fought it out among themselves.

Another hazard was illness. In spite of daily doses of huge anti-malarial pills, John managed to get it. After a week in the local army hospital he discharged himself to take a wedding looking most peculiar. He was entirely yellow from the medication which made him look like a zombie in his white cassock. Michael stayed remarkably well in Nanyuki with only the occasional tummy upset. Her recurrent illness in those early months was tonsillitis. For weeks she suffered from an infected throat and enlarged glands. This was just before the advent of penicillin so she devised her own cure. Mendl's Throat Paint was a viscous black liquid with which one was supposed to dab those nasty little white spots with a proper paint brush, a procedure guaranteed to make anyone gag. She discovered that it acted much more quickly if she gargled with it. In desperation she gargled non-stop for a week, going through three bottles by which time she reckoned she had killed her tonsils. Certainly she never got tonsillitis again.

But there were other happier occasions. They hosted a reel party on the grass outside the rondavels dancing Eightsomes and Dashing White Sergeants on the grass to gramophone records with the car headlights turned on. Together with Michael they often explored a nearby stream which sparkled through tall trees and reminded her of burns in Scotland. She began to dress-make from material bought from one of the Nanyuki shops. The Army lent her a treadle sewing machine and Mother sent her Vogue patterns from home. Nothing quite fitted but the fabric was not rationed. She experimented with foods that were new to her such as corn-on-the-cob which preceded most dinner parties, mangoes and pawpaws with lemon juice for breakfast. Thuko did most of the food marketing and no doubt made himself a small profit. If so, good for him. She was ashamed of the fact that the meat provided by employers for their African servants, and known as 'boys' meat', consisted of the cheaper cuts and 'posho' which was a sort of maize porridge.

They played a lot of music on their gramophone and John introduced her to composers she had hardly heard of. She particularly liked Prokofiev's *Classical Symphony*. He gave her the whole of Handel's *Messiah*, some thirty odd records, for Christmas. (Sadly the records were all to get warped in the trunk during the voyage home back to Britain.) She started to write short stories again, and even sent them to Argosy, an upmarket magazine which published only the best. That was the start of the rejection slips. By the time she finally found a publisher years later she could have papered a room with them. She made friends among the other wives, gossiped and entertained.

Her time at Nanyuki lasted no longer than a year. John, who by now had a motor-bike for transport, (she had only once dared to ride on the back and nearly died of terror) came home one day to tell her he had been posted to Mogadishu, Mussolini's show colonial city in what had once been Italian Somaliland.

For some reason John was needed there immediately while she and Michael were left to travel more leisurely from Mombasa on board the *SS EMPIRE KEN*. This entailed three or four days in the Nyali Transit Camp to await her passage along with the dozens of other families on their way home. One of these was a fellow officer from Nanyuki with his ten-year old son whose wife had been flown home in a hurry to attend a dying parent. It was with Iain and his son, Colin, that she was to have her scariest adventure.

The beach was safe and sheltered from sharks by a coral reef about half a mile from the shore. Strong swimmers came back with tales of its wonders so Iain suggested they hire one of the local dug-out canoes with two Africans to row, and explore it for themselves. The water was a bit choppy but the Africans assured them it was safe. Unfortunately a squall arose when they were about midway to the reef. Before she had time to feel scared the boat had capsized and all of them, including eighteen-month old Michael, found themselves adrift in a lukewarm sea.

The boat had not completely sunk. It lay upside down, submerged under about a half a foot of water, but still something to clutch on to with one hand while she held Michael aloft in her other arm and treaded water with her legs. To her horror she saw Iain and his son, who at ten, was a strong swimmer, strike out for shore. Neither of the two Africans could swim so they too clutched fearfully on to the wreck. She heard herself cry out 'Don't leave me,' and he had shouted back 'Going to get help.'

It was the longest half-hour of her life. Michael, on the other hand, thought it all a huge game. He ducked her head under water and shrieked with laughter every time she re-emerged. They had of course been spotted for the beach was busy that day and Iain soon returned, full of apologies, with another boat, though it had been none of his fault. The other families made a huge fuss of her and she got a little drunk that night.

Mogadishu was a beautiful city. When the Italians had surrendered, their part of Somalia was temporarily taken over by the British government who administered it like any other British colony with a District Commissioner and a Chief Administrator at the top and all the other officials downwards with six regiments to keep order, to whom John was both chaplain and padre.

Their quarter was one of many built by Mussolini for his army families in a huge double tenement next door to a mosque overlooking the sea and known as the Mediterranean Flats. They were superb. Marble floors, high ceilings with fans, spacious rooms with a huge fridge in the dining room and a proper kitchen, all sparsely but adequately furnished. John had acquired from the previous tenant two Somali servants, Mohammed and Hassan, clever, handsome young men who not only could cook but also could speak four languages, Somali, Italian, Swahili and English.

Social life was a giddy whirl from coffee mornings to cocktail parties, beach picnics to Sunday lunches, dinner parties to tennis. Ah tennis...

There was not much love lost between the Brits and the Italian settlers at the best of times but on the tennis courts the atmosphere became vicious. No doubt the British women who played during the daytime behaved badly. They arrogantly thought that the Italians - they were all young men - should give way to them. Those young wives expected them to give up their games and their courts more or less on demand and Betty was no better than the others. The disgruntled Italians would sit in the pavilion and make disparaging remarks about the women. Betty, who was taking Italian lessons from the local priest, could not fail to understand '*Quella visagio!*' She knew at once that they were referring to her scarlet face for day-time tennis was excruciatingly hot.

At John's request, they held open house on Tuesday afternoons for the other ranks and Thursdays for the young officers who had very little else to amuse themselves as so much of the city was out of bounds and under curfew at that time. Six men from each regiment, eighteen at a time, came to play games such as Monopoly, chess, rummy, do jigsaws or just talk and play with Michael. They were all National Servicemen. Socially they were a mixture from viscount to crossing sweeper in civilian life but they all had two things in common, youth and homesickness. Mohammed served them with his delicious homemade limeade, ice-cold from the fridge, and Hassan made biscuits and cakes.

Of the six regiments she was involved mostly with the Duke of Cornwall's Light Infantry. DCLI wives occupied many of the other flats and she made particular friends with one, Inge, a German wife, who looked after Michael when she and John had a night off to go out for a meal or visit the open-air cinema. The films were all in Italian and she particularly remembered watching the bats flit across the screen during the brilliant and unforgettable *Bicycle Thief.*

Meanwhile John had been asked to play the piano in a small jazz band and she had been given a part in a somewhat suggestive sketch in a revue called *No Names* in which she took the role of a posh maid to a coarse madam and had to ask for a glass of 'Fullabulsh' and other similarly named concoctions for her mistress. This brought shouts of laughter and stamps of applause from the male audience. Later John had to explain why. But she was given a DCLI regimental brooch in appreciation of her sportsmanship.

Sunday curry lunches after church parade were rather grand affairs. The first one she attended was hosted by one of the colonels in his spacious quarter. The curry was absolutely delicious. Dozens of little side dishes with a few recognisable things like banana and coconut and just as many she had never before tasted. Because she had drunk too much wine, she made the terrible mistake of having a second helping. She was the only one and it seemed to her as if everyone else round the table was watching her with amusement as she poured with sweat and struggled to finish. The pudding was something smooth and cool and creamy and she would have liked a second helping of that too but it wasn't offered. After they had eaten and drunk, the host allocated everyone a bedroom to sleep it off.

One of the older officer's wives in the 14/20th Kings Hussars decided to take her under her wing. She was a terrifying woman with a double-barrelled name and she would summon Betty round to her home to play Poker Patience. 'Call me Dibs,' she insisted but Betty never summoned up the courage. Dibs also decided that both she and John must learn to play bridge. The lessons were slow and painful especially where John was concerned for he was no card lover. Finally the day came when they were to be launched on the bridge-playing community. The first rubber was to be played against Dibs and her husband, the Major. John, whose confidence was precariously high, made the mistake of doubling her bid of four spades (He had five in his hand so it was understandable) but which she got with no trouble at all. 'Fifty for insult,' she informed him calmly as she totted up the score.

John turned scarlet. Not realising this was a standard bridge score, he really thought he had insulted her. He refused to play bridge again. Betty's mother had told her that her father had always refused to learn bridge seeing it as decidedly not part of a priest's requirements. Remembering this, Betty, who rather liked bridge, did not argue. She played a lot of bridge on the voyage home and lost a bit of money. (She was never much good at the game either.)

Alcohol was cheap and terrifyingly prevalent especially on Mess nights. John hated it even more than he hated bridge, the smell and the taste of spirits in particular. His father had been strictly teetotal during his years as manager of the Shanghai Electric Company for the same reason. Drink was too cheap and too easily available to the British community. He had therefore as a young man 'signed the pledge'. So John too decided that he would be teetotal. He wasn't, of course. No priest can be entirely teetotal. Mess nights were therefore a cross which he was forced to bear. He had no trouble in the NAAFI or in the Sergeants' Mess where he sat down at the piano and played one request after another and had them all singing happily while he nursed a glass of coke.

Michael celebrated his second birthday with a big party in the flat, lots of other children, various army and civilian wives and a big cake. Hassan's young wife shrouded from head to foot in Muslim black came to the door to offer a bush-baby as a gift for Michael. Betty would have accepted it had John not put his foot down. He already knew what she had not yet been told that the women and children were all to be evacuated either home to Britain or back to Kenya. Italian Somaliland was to be formally handed over to the United Nations and more trouble was expected from the Somalis who hated the eight o'clock curfew and the fact that their country was yet again to be occupied, so the army was on full alert.

A fortnight later she was back on board ship heading for Nyali Transit Camp again where she and a number of other families were to wait for their husbands to join them after the transfer. As she was now a permanent resident she was given two furnished rooms in one of the grander Nissen huts and after the trauma of losing Michael while she was unpacking - he had wandered off by himself to the African quarters - decided to follow the example of other resident wives and employ an ayah.

Adeja was a pretty young woman married to one of the African servants. She did Michael's washing and took him to play on the beach with the other children and their ayahs and baby-sat in the evening while she dined in the Mess and socialised. Soon he was jabbering away in Swahili, as were all the other small children.

It was a strange existence and rather spoiled by the fact that she got kidney stones and had to be hospitalised on two short occasions while Michael with Adeja was looked after by one of the other wives. Then Michael got a mild form of malaria and he too had to spend a few days in hospital. Fortunately John joined them after some two months, and, as he was posted to Mackinnon Road, a station midway between Mombasa and Nairobi, she stayed on at Nyali where he joined her for two days midweek.

During those last few months in Nyali on the days when she was well, she was able to go for day long walks sometimes with John, sometimes with other transients mostly north up the coast line. She saw cliffs with the fossilised remains of great animals which might well have been dinosaurs embedded in their strata, encountered a pack of hyena running along the sands, and bathed naked in remote sandy bays. She made a host of new friends, sun-bathed in the heat of the day and both she and Michael got as brown as beech mast. Dancing in the evening ended somewhat abruptly when a black mamba got inside the radiogram and broke it. The snake was beaten to death by an African waiter but the radiogram never recovered. Instead those with the stamina (and a bit of money) walked the mile or so along the shore to the Nyali Beach Hotel which had a small live band, a proper dance floor and excellent cuisine. She and John went once.

All too soon John's three-year posting was up and it was time to go back to Scotland. He was offered another African tour of three years but sadly for them all, he had to refuse because Betty needed to get back to have those painful kidney stones attended to.

Reflections

'Show me an African who doesn't believe in God,' someone once said and it was true. They were hard to find. John loved and was invigorated by his ministry to the KAR (King's African Rifles), and their families. He learned enough Swahili to be able to take their services and preach short simple sermons without the constant use of an interpreter.

I too liked the Africans but not, I think, as fellow human beings. I was still half-way between the opinion of many of the settlers who considered them to be a sub-species and John who was completely non-racist. I would never have been rude or cruel or even unpleasant but then I would never have been rude, cruel or unpleasant to Oor Wullie. I know this because of how I felt when John invited a black pastor to afternoon tea. Although I was probably - hopefully - polite, I felt distinctly uncomfortable seeing him lean back in one of our easy chairs and eat cake as if this were normal. Though of course it should have been, it was not *de rigeur* in the Kenya of 1948. I knew that our landlady, Mrs R, and most of our new friends would have had forty fits and this mattered to me in those days. I looked at the plain little man with enormous white buck-teeth talking and laughing with John both entirely at their ease. Or so I thought. I was aware of his smell just as, so I was later informed, he would have been aware of and disgusted by mine. It is likely that he too felt uncomfortable in the company of this silent white woman, who, by her body language, if not her words, made him feel unwelcome. No surprise that the Mau Mau freedom fighters were already on the prowl. The wonder is that the Africans I knew, including that laughing, black pastor and Thuko who I was content to call 'boy', were so pleasant, so forgiving, so good-tempered.

I reached some sort of nadir in my attitude towards racial issues at that tea party. Afterwards when John rightly and strongly criticised my behaviour, which he had instantly recognised, I was ashamed of myself. I can date a shift in my attitude towards Africans from that afternoon. Although I still saw the British as God's chosen people, I began to see blacks as human beings on a par with French or American, for instance, just a little lower than Scots on the human scale. Germans were somewhere near the bottom, but that stupid belief had already faded. Probably my best friend in Mogadishu was my close neighbour, Inge, the young German wife of one of the DCLI officers. She had few other friends and the reason was obvious. We never spoke about the war but she taught me how to make a proper applestrudel.

I did not often get to church in Kenya. John disappeared early on Sunday mornings and did not return until late in the evening and I had Michael to care for. There was a small Anglican Church in Nanyuki whose vicar had the unfortunate name of Crook. He and his wife were friendly and memorable mostly because of the nest of snakes that somehow managed to hatch out in one of their wardrobes, but I seldom saw them.

In Mogadishu there was a compulsory church parade most Sundays held in the vast open space below our block of flats. Two young soldiers were detailed to look after Michael so that I could attend these services with the other wives, and impressive they were. One of the bands played for the hymns and officers read the lessons, flags were in evidence and the men sang their hearts out. John wore a white cassock under his white surplice, his Durham university hood and a broad black scarf with the Chaplain Department's elaborate badge of an equal-armed cross and the motto 'In this sign I conquer,' embroidered near the foot of it. He loved that scarf and wore it at Matins and Evensong long after he had retired from the army.

Sitting at the back, I was amused by the number of buttons that found their way into the alms dish and I actually saw a young soldier put in a sixpence and fish around for a threepenny bit. I don't suppose I put in more than a shilling myself. I don't think I got out of the habit of giving a shilling or even a sixpence for many years to come. In Old St Pauls it had mostly been a penny.

Nor do I remember thinking much about God in those days. It must have been about then that I started to take comfort in the idea that as long as John served God faithfully I was safe, whatever that meant. I could enjoy myself, drink a bit too much, gossip, flirt a little, party late, but as long as John kept up the Christian bit I would come to no harm spiritually speaking. I still knelt at my side of the bed to say my evening prayers but they did not amount to much, a quick thank you, a slightly longer 'God bless... ' a gabbled Lord's Prayer and a further few seconds wondering if I had spent long enough on my knees. I was in bed and well into my book before John finished.

Back at Nyali there were no Sunday services to go to in the transit camp and I got used to not going to church. When John came back midweek we would occasionally say Evensong together when Michael was asleep, and he would hold a midweek communion service for the few in the camp that wanted it to which I usually went while Michael was safe with Adeja. As he had no study in Nyali, I would join the other wives on the beach in the mornings to give him space to say his office and write his sermons.

Had anyone asked me at that time if I believed in God, I would have replied indignantly 'of course,' but there was little evidence of it in my daily life. I took God and my faith entirely for granted.

Chapter Four

Church Crookham

They sailed back on the SS EMPIRE TEST and this time had a cabin to themselves. Her first impression of Britain in early May was the startling variations of green everywhere. Spring in the Black Isle is breathtakingly beautiful, glorious yellow from whin and broom and carpets of dandelions, every shade of green from the bottle of pine to the feathery emerald of larch, and every shade of blue and silver from the encircling sky and sea. The Black Isle is never black. After the sands and plains of Kenya she discovered its rainbow beauty all over again.

In Fortrose there had been changes. Bunty was now married to a tea planter and had just had her first baby in Ceylon, Florence was reading philosophy at St Andrews University. Betty's godmother, Aunt Sine, had moved away and Mother had made new friends. After the usual whirl of tea and supper parties including the occasional bridge evening, they enjoyed a few days at the Edinburgh Festival now into its second year. They managed to fill every available moment with concerts and Betty particularly enjoyed the spectacle of Lindsay's *Three Estates (Ane Pleasant Satyre of the Thrie Estaits)* performed in the Assembly Rooms. She also had a beauty treatment at Jenners, the first and only one in her life, and wasted rather a lot of money on a spectacular black ball dress which she wore once because it never really fitted across the bust. Meanwhile John heard that they had been allotted an army quarter; 23 Wakefield Copse, in a village called Church Crookham not far from Aldershot, where he had been posted as Chaplain to the Royal Army Medical Corps depot.

Church Crookham, too, was a beautiful place. The copse, across the road from the little circular estate of army houses, was alive with nightingales and the countryside - most of it wild and owned by the army where tanks practised whatever tanks do - wonderful for walks.

Here she experienced army life at its best, close, convivial and busy. She took down her bicycle, added a child seat to the back for Michael and biked everywhere, to the NAAFI for groceries, to neighbours for coffee, to the village where she took Michael to dancing lessons. She made new friends and found old ones. Sheila and Jimmy had been in Nanyuki and had Christopher who was Michael's age.

Sheila was a sporty person who decided that they should get up a women's cricket eleven and challenge an army team. Enthusiastically backed by Jimmy and John who fancied himself as a wicket keeper, twelve suitable women were duly persuaded or dragooned into a team. The army tailors made them fetching little outfits consisting of shorts and top all-in-one in a tough white cotton (she was to wear it for many tennis years to follow) and they were coached by one of the sergeants who was impressed by Sheila who was a star but not by Betty, who, because she had played cricket (and hated it) at school, thought she knew it all. The Saturday of the match duly arrived, cloudless, and the ground was crowded with families, all ranks eager to see the sergeants mess second eleven well and truly beaten.

As first bat, she walked proudly up to the wicket accompanied by whistles and catcalls to take the first ball. The young bowler not knowing what he was facing gave it his best shot. (He was county player) The ball came hurtling down like a bullet out of the blue. Scared stiff she took a step sideways and it crashed on the wicket sending the bails flying. If it was any comfort, the whole team was out for 11 runs most of them made by Sheila and it took all of twenty minutes. It was hastily decided to start again and this time the sergeants would play left-handed. Their condescension was unbearable. This time she made three runs before being bowled out and the overall score was in the 30s. The sergeants retired at 50 runs one man down, bowled out by a slow daisy-cutter. But it was a fun afternoon. The men were unbearably smug but their wives produced a sumptuous tea.

Christopher and Michael both aged four roamed freely between the houses and in the copse. On one memorable occasion while she and John were entertaining two National Servicemen who were both training for the ministry in civilian life, the little boys disappeared as usual. Tea was an awkward occasion. The two young men, earnest and evangelical, sat at the edges of their chairs while she poured tea and John tried not to be hearty. Suddenly the sitting room door crashed open and two little lads, naked and smeared all over with bramble juice burst into the room waving sticks intended to be tomahawks crying, 'Walla walla wooskie, damn-blast-bloody! Walla walla wooskie, damn-blast-bloody.'

The young men were horrified. John rose sternly, Betty's jaw dropped. Seeing their faces, the two little boys fled. John and Betty badly wanted to laugh but one glimpse at the young men's faces told them this was no laughing matter. They left with disapproval written large on their faces. Meanwhile the children had both disappeared. They were eventually found by a neighbour hiding in his tool shed.

Young men training for the ministry usually ended up as John's batmen. They soon became part of the family, not only sharing meals but in several cases, cooking them too. The worst job in those army quarters was trying to keep the brown composition floors clean. One scuff of a black shoe and they were dirty again. The only way to clean them was down on your knees with a scrubbing brush then polishing with a large heavy bumper. The batmen were in charge of the bumper.

Watching the young medics square-bashing fascinated Michael so they would stop and stare on their way to the NAAFI shop where she bought all her groceries and gossiped with the other wives. It was exactly like one of the Fortrose stores only bigger. There was also a paper shop opposite and on Tuesday and Thursday afternoons a queue of young soldiers trailed round the square. She found out later that they were Beano and Dandy publication days.

One of their neighbours was a relative of the writer Maurice Walsh. She never got to know him well but she was very much in awe of someone who was related however distantly to a real writer. It spurred her on. She had now realised that handwritten manuscripts were unprofessional (and in her case illegible) so John bought her a portable typewriter in exchange for typing his sermons. It was a neat little machine in a leather case but she had not a clue how to use it. Her next assignment would be to learn to type. She bought a *Teach Yourself* handbook, tied the strings of her apron round her neck, draped the skirt over the keys and began at the beginning. It worked because she was determined to make it work. To begin with, her typing was as careless and illegible as her handwriting but gradually her fingers learned what to do. Proudly she produced one of John's sermons but it was so inaccurate that he never asked her again. However she persevered. Later when she was producing full length manuscripts she would allow herself no more than three errors per page carefully typexed out. The most tiresome mistake was putting the blue carbon sheets in the wrong way round. It happened more often than she would have believed possible usually when she was late and tired. Although her short stories were plentiful, publication eluded her and the rejection slips piled up.

Captain and Mrs H, next-door neighbours on one side, an older childless couple, took a kindly interest in them all. Shortly after their arrival in Church Crookham her kidney stone decided to move. The pain was so excruciating that she could only scream. Michael was taken next door to Mrs H while John sent for the doctor. She was whipped into the Princess Louise Margaret Hospital for women in Aldershot. Under anaesthetic the surgeon identified the stone but could not get at it to remove it. As the pain had stopped she was sent home and told to skip and drink plenty of water in the hopes that it would pass naturally. It did. In Buckingham Palace loo. They had gone up to London which was only an hour's train journey away to see the see the royal pictures on exhibition, and, for the first time in a couple of years she was free from that annoying little pain which had spoiled her last months in East Africa.

Mary, their neighbour on the other side was Irish and Catholic and had four children. On Monday nights while the two husbands baby sat, she and Mary went to the pictures by bus to the nearest town, Fleet. Afterwards they stopped for fish and chips before catching the bus home. In October 1951 she was pregnant again, heavily pregnant, the baby due in a week's time, when they went to see *It's a Mad Mad Mad Mad World*. She laughed so much that her waters broke on the way home. Mary who had been a nurse ordered an ambulance and she was whipped into the Louise Margaret Hospital once again and Jeremy was born in the early hours of the following morning. It was an unbelievably easy birth for she had been given gas and air, a miracle invention which had not been available for Michael. The only hitch came at the actual moment of birth. 'Stop pushing,' the midwife ordered in the sort of voice that even a half-born baby obeyed. Minutes later she was told to push again. The cord had been round the infant's neck but the midwife had freed it in time.

To her incredulity the baby was another boy. So sure had she been that it would be a girl that she had already picked out the name, Veronica. Neither of them could think of a suitable boy's name and John was no help. He did not mind so long as it was Christian in the strictest sense of the word. A parcel had arrived from her godmother containing a hand-knit baby jacket and a book for Michael. *The Tale of Jeremy Fisher.* All babies look a little like frogs don't they? Anyhow that was how he got his name.

In 1951, ten days was the minimum stay in hospital after the birth of a baby. The ward was huge, ten beds, but the babies were kept apart in a nursery and brought in, labelled and laid out on trolleys, at four hourly intervals for feeding. A baby was duly handed to her. She put down the book she had been reading, unwound the tightly wrapped shawl and yelled. The baby was completely yellow and nothing resembling her frog. Simultaneously there was a scream from the other end of the ward. 'This is not my baby.' But supposing neither of them had noticed? What a nightmare. But of course they did. Jeremy was swiftly rescued and the yellow gnome returned to its rightful owner.

As a chaplain's wife, not much was required of her apart from entertaining the ordination candidates among the National Servicemen at least not until the Grand Summer Fete, not an annual event, thank heavens, but dreamed up by the senior officers in aid of SSAFA, the forces charity, to be organised by the chaplain. The stalls and sideshows were taken over by the various units and she deputed to look after Lady M, a local VIP who had been corralled into opening the Fete. All Betty had to do was organise the presentation of a bouquet and take her round the stalls.

It was a very grand affair, packed out with villagers and visitors as well as the whole depot. Bunting flew merrily, races were run, coconut shies, bran tubs and fancy goods stalls did a brisk trade. Lady M duly arrived accompanied by an escort of high-heid-yins. The C-in-C introduced her ladyship who duly and graciously said a few appropriate words. One of Mary's pretty children in a pink party dress presented her with a spectacular bouquet of flowers and then it was Betty's turn.

'Perhaps these could be kept in water until I leave?' Lady M said handing Betty the flowers. She took them to the obvious place, the flower stall, and put them in a bucket of water with strict injunctions to look after them. Then she escorted the great lady round the stalls where she generously spent a lot of money. The purchases were handed to Betty, jams, cakes, baby-knits, raffle tickets. Lady M, not a new-comer to these events, had fortunately brought a couple of shopping bags which were full by the time the colonel and his wife came to escort her to the tea tent. Betty took the bags back to the waiting car, handed them over to the chauffeur and went off to the flower stall to recover the bouquet. Horrors! It was nowhere to be seen. The stall had sold out and most of the helpers had already left. Someone had obviously sold it but no one would admit to the deed. Oh God, what to do now. She hurried round the Fete to see if she could spot the flowers on someone's arm, but they were nowhere to be seen. The crowds had thinned considerably. No one knew anything. They had literally vanished. On dragging feet she returned to the tea tent to explain what had happened. Lady M had, however, already left. Betty was just in time to see the colonel waving her car off the sports field.

Now what to do? She decided she had better write so John said he would get hold of Lady M's address on Monday morning.

Later that evening, however, the telephone rang. It was Lady M. 'My dear, I am so sorry!' she gushed. 'What must you think of me? I forgot all about my pretty flowers.'

So Betty confessed. Lady M laughed and soon Betty was laughing too. 'I am so glad you made some money out of them. I can't tell you how relieved I am. I was dreading having to tell you.'

But of course it was really Betty's fault. It was not a mistake that she would ever make again. But there was another one which was much worse. Jeremy's baptism.

Finding a godmother was only too easy, though Tricia was in South Africa at the time and could not attend the Christening. John insisted that there were two godfathers. Bill was an army friend and happy to agree. Meanwhile, after much thought, she wrote to Uncle Bob. Never thinking that he would come, she left it a bit late. The little ceremony in the small army chapel was over by the time his reply came. He would like to be a godfather and he and Aunt Nell would be happy to attend the service. When would it be and where would it be held? She had forgotten that Uncle Bob was still a serving officer, a Brigadier in the Royal Artillery. No doubt he was curious to visit the RAMC depot. How was she to explain that the service had been held the previous Saturday? She even suggested to John that the ceremony be held all over again. That was how desperate she felt. However Uncle Bob was forgiving. He admitted to finding it a little odd but he would still consider himself to be a godfather and Aunt Nell sent Jeremy a romper suit, much the best bit of clothing he ever possessed.

During those last few months John had a big decision to make. His six years army commission was up. He had been offered the chance to extend it for another six years. If he chose to stay, his next posting would be to Germany. However much he was tempted, he was aware that army life with its regulated Padre's Hours and batmen and proper office was not for him. Happy though he continued to be in the NAAFI with the other ranks or in the sergeants' mess and with no money worries on an annual income of £600 and rising, he was ill-at-ease with his fellow officers and did not understand or enjoy the conviviality of the officers' mess. He wanted the familiarity of parish life with 'high' churchmanship preferable, 'middle-of the-road' if necessary but not the 'low' of the little RAMC chapel in the depot.

The decision made, the future unknown, she received a letter a few days later from her friend Bar, whose father had been the

Chaplain General and was now Dean of Ripon Cathedral. 'Daddy's looking for a minor canon. Would John be interested?'

John was. An English cathedral with all that wonderful music! It was beyond a dream. Three months later in a bleak November they left Church Crookham and army life for good.

Reflections

Would I have liked John to stay on in the army? I can't remember. In those days clergy wives did not make decisions or even have too many opinions where priestly vocations were concerned. John did not feel he had a true calling to army life, and I respected that. Basically a shy person and a non-drinker, he often felt out of his depths, especially on the social side. He made the right decision for him and never regretted it. But he stayed on in the Territorial Army which involved summer camps anywhere in the British Isles and these he thoroughly enjoyed.

Ever an optimist, I never had any doubts that all would be ultimately be well and so it was. Ripon cathedral, for heaven's sake. Thank you, God.

But those three years in Church Crookham were happy and fulfilling times. I now had two little boys. How wonderful was that. We had made friends, had an adequate income and a lot of fun. Spiritually speaking, I began for the first time tentatively to think for myself both about my faith and about the wider church.

My personal concern was over the Prayer of Humble Access which comes in the Communion service. '... Grant us...to eat the flesh of thy dear son Jesus Christ, and to drink his blood....' I had repeated it Sunday by Sunday with only small reservations since my Confirmation, but now the reservations became important. 'High Church' insisted that Transubstantiation took place. The bread and wine literally became the body and blood of Christ. For about a year, I suppose, I just stopped saying the words that seemed such blatant cannibalism. Then I heard myself say to Jeremy, a tiny baby at that time, 'You are so gorgeous I could just eat you up!' and that stopped me short. I had finally made sense of the words. They were metaphor and they were to do with love. The bread and the wine literally became the body and blood of Christ for me, had the same effect on me as if I had taken Christ 'under my roof'. Metaphor and mystery. That prayer which begins 'We do not presume...' became one of the few I could and can repeat word for word from memory, one of my many prayer book favourites.

My other concern was more general. I was visited and befriended by an elderly villager, Miss J, who told me that that as a parson's wife I ought to be enrolled into the Mothers Union. 'Every parish worth its salt has an MU, and, as often as not, you, as the vicar's wife, will be expected to lead it, so take my advice and let me get you enrolled.' It sounded sensible.

I knew very little about the MU. Although it most certainly had - and has - a Scottish presence, it is at heart an Anglican organisation with its headquarters at Mary Sumner House in London. It could be likened to the Scottish Women's Guild which supports Presbyterian congregations throughout Scotland. In Dundee I remember the Mother's Meeting which my own mother attended from time to time but it never had the influence over the parish that the MU had in England in general, and, in particular, Church Crookham.

It did strike me as a little odd that a maiden lady should not only be a member of the MU, but also the Enrolling Member, (who corresponded to the chairman or president of other organisations), but I was glad. It seemed an inclusive thing to do. It was only when one of the other wives in the housing scheme told me that she was excluded because she had been divorced that I realised that the MU in those days was far from inclusive. Not only did it exclude divorced mothers but also unmarried mothers. The Anglican church was no better, though. It barred divorcees from the sacrament, and, in those days, to be an unmarried mother was a matter of shame. I did query this in a half-hearted sort of way with Miss J. 'Why call it a Mothers Union if some mothers are barred?' but she brushed it aside. 'Good gracious me! You don't expect to belong to a choir unless you can sing,' she said. 'Those are the rules. The MU has rules too.' I pretended I saw the sense of this because I was still very immature and unconfident in my own judgements. I attended as many of the weekly meetings in the Church Hall as possible, which were not that many, saw for myself that its aims and most of its regulations were helpful and its members friendly and sincere. So I duly became enrolled by the vicar with a blue veil tied round my head. Indeed I was grateful to Miss J. When it came to the time when I would inherit a large and powerful MU, I knew when to break what were fast becoming outdated and unpleasant rules which now no longer exist. In the MU of today all mums, thankfully, are equally welcome.

Chapter Five

Ripon Cathedral

They moved in November 1952. Betty and Michael went ahead to meet the furniture. Jeremy and John stayed behind to hand back the house to the army, bunking down with their long-suffering next-door neighbours for a night or two.

The accommodation at Ripon was 'quaint' to put it kindly. The servants' quarters of what had been the old Deanery, now remodelled into a hotel, were rickety and cockroach-infested. The upstairs and main part of the flat was built over a conglomeration of what had once been coach houses and was now a combination of garages and storage sheds; the downstairs dining room and kitchen had been part of the original back quarters of the old Deanery. There was a cobbled courtyard and a tiny walled garden outside at the front. At the back was Mr Lickiss' market garden. Inside and up a narrow rickety wooden staircase, there were four rooms with low ceilings, a sitting room, a small study, a small bedroom for themselves, a slightly larger bedroom for the two boys, and, down three steps, a tiny bathroom. The Dean had seen to it that the whole place was repainted and seemingly in working order. She was charmed before she found out that every chimney in the small fireplaces smoked and then there were the cockroaches.

They had spent John's army gratuity on two extravagant items, a made-to-measure red carpet ordered from Waring and Gillow's in London and a television set which cost at that time the princely and prohibitive sum of £60. In retrospect it was a foolish splurge. Their income which had been an adequate £600 pa in the army was now down to £250 plus a third share of the Easter Offering (about £20). They could have done with that army gratuity, although, as she argued with herself, it would have just been frittered away on the weekly housekeeping. The red wall-to-wall carpet, which she had set her heart on and which was to grace every rectory thereafter, was never a success. It showed up every thread and speck of dust and required a lot more sweeping than the ancient carpets that had been acquired by her grandmother some fifty years earlier in India.

The television, on the other hand, was her delight. They were the only people she knew to have television. Not even Mr Dean and Mrs Hughes had television and she and Michael would watch the activities of Mr Bean (Benny Hill) and his Mean Machine in raptures. John never much cared for it apart from Motor Racing and the News. It really came into its own for the Coronation the following June when everyone turned up to watch it in her little sitting room.

'Everyone' in Ripon consisted of the Dean and Mrs Hughes, Bar on her short breaks from nursing, Dilys, their younger daughter now at university who spent her holidays at home, three residentiary canons including Canon Bartlett and his wife, an elderly priest famed for his knowledge of and friendship with the Romanies (he would not tolerate the word gypsies) and three married minor canons, one of whom, Carlos, was to become John's special buddy.

Although John was in constant touch with the other clergy for they had weekly staff meetings, she saw little of the other minor canons' wives. Each of them was busy with small children and each had her own small niche in the life of the parish but there was a solidarity between them never more in evidence than with the tramps. There seemed to be a lot of them around in the early fifties. One particularly regular old reprobate called Ollie would turn up at Betty's door. He would be offered and often accepted a cup of tea and a sandwich, but it was money he was after. Betty would suggest he try Duncan's wife, Stefana. She too would offer him tea and perhaps an old shirt or jumper, but, as she had no money either, she would suggest he try Carlos and Mary. They would send him straight to the Dean who always gave him cash. It passed a happy and profitable morning for Ollie, became a talking point for the three wives and it happened about once a month.

She saw far more of the Dean and his family for the Deanery - a vast Victorian barn - was very close. Mrs Hughes was gently generous, a mother figure to her and another grandmother to Michael who was a great favourite. She saw Mrs Hughes most days. Sometimes she would drive Betty and the two boys out for picnics to near-by Fountains Abbey where the children threw stones into the river or ran around the wonderful ruins. They would be invited to Christmas lunch when Dilys and Bar, Betty's particular friend, would both be there and the Dean at his sparkling best.

When Dilys was away at university Betty would be summoned to play tennis with Mr Dean. She would wear her white outfit made for that fatal cricket match in Church Crookham and he would appear in white flannels. Michael, now five, was ball boy for which the Dean paid him a penny a set while Jeremy, strapped into his pushchair, patiently watched. He was, on the whole, a very patient child. The Dean would stand in the middle of his court and considered it poor sportsmanship unless Betty sent the ball directly to him. He did not like to lose and he never did. Playing with Dilys was a different matter. Having just watched Wimbledon on television, they decided to try running in to the net after serving. The trouble was that their serves (when they were in) were usually too weak to merit a run-in and during most of the games they collapsed in laughter. She did a lot of giggling in those days; on no occasion so terrible as the night the Dean entertained Montie.

Dean Hughes was a personal friend of General Montgomery. (Indeed it was on his recommendation that he was to become Chaplain General, or so it was said.) Montie decided to pay a personal visit to his friend Freddie, so Mr Dean invited the three minor canons and their wives to dinner to entertain the great man. The dinner went well. Conversation flowed. Montie advised them all to put their sons' names down for Leatherhead public school where he was a governor and offered to put in a good word for them. After dinner it was up to the younger men to offer some entertainment. For John it was easy, a sing-song of army tunes. Montie joined in and approved. Carlos who had no skills in that direction was excused but Duncan who was a classical musician sang an Italian love song in a rather reedy counter tenor. She caught Dilys' eye. Oh the agony of trying to suppress laughter! It happened from time to time, usually in church, but this was a very grown-up dinner party. Her eyes watered, she spluttered and tried to pass it off as a cough. Dilys disappeared. Fortunately Montie and the Dean were older and kinder and Duncan was congratulated and called 'a good chap'.

Apart from Mrs Hughes, she came into little contact with the cathedral hierarchy and their families. Mrs Bartlett, however, was determined to train her up to be a useful clergy wife. First and foremost she must set a good example to the other young wives. This meant attending the new 9.30 Family Eucharist with both children. No leaving Jeremy with the baby sitter, Betty Lickiss, whose father ran the market garden in what had been the old Deanery gardens.

So the following Sunday she duly turned up with Michael and Jeremy in the pushchair. He slept for most of the service and was still asleep when it was time to go up to the communion rails. He must have woken to find her gone. His wails echoed and re-echoed round the vast stone building. If you have never heard a child cry in a cathedral you don't know what noise is. She rushed back, seized the pram and ran the length of the nave with Michael flying behind her. Never again.

One of John's jobs was chaplain to the Cathedral Youth Club. When she was asked to open their annual summer sale she could think of no good reason to refuse. Being terrified of public speaking was not a viable excuse. She wrote out a neat little speech on the back on an envelope, as she had been advised to do, and learned it by heart. She practised it in the bath, to her long-suffering children, made John hear it again and again until she was word perfect. What could go wrong? The Saturday eventually arrived. She put on her best dress and was duly welcomed on to the hall platform while the crowds hushed expectantly and she launched into the familiar words. Half-way through and over-confident, she could see the door at the far end of the hall open and the Dean came in. He waved and called out a greeting. That was it. She forgot her lines. Her hesitation extended into an awkward pause. One of the younger members of the Youth Club was pushed forwards and she was presented with a bunch of exotic orchids. (The child's father was a florist) She had just enough presence of mind to accept graciously (she hoped) and declare the sale open. The press photographers were there to record that heart-stopping moment for posterity.

Fund-raising events, jumble sales, raffles, fetes not only for the Cathedral took every spare penny. The only raffle she ever won in those days was a cake which had been donated in aid of SSAFA. The beautifully decorated confection sat in a shop window for several weeks before the draw. Word came that she had won it. Great excitement as with Michael and Jeremy she plunged in the knife. It was rotten. The cake was full of green mould. That was the beginning of a long experience of disappointing raffle wins. Once she won two pillow-cases that she had herself donated because she disliked them. On another occasion she won a huge supply of meat in the days before freezers. It had to be picked up on the Saturday after the sale and eaten on Sunday. An impossible task. It had been a hot weekend and the meat was already slightly off. What the refuse collectors made of the stink in her dust-bin she was never to find out as their annual holiday had started on the Monday.

She was also talked into becoming Brown Owl for the Cathedral Brownie pack. She enjoyed this and taught the children to sing and act *The Wee Cooper of Fife*, which they performed at the Sunday School Annual Concert.

It was Florence who discovered the cockroaches. A student at St Andrews, she had come to stay for a few days that first spring. The spare bed was a Put-u-Up sofa which they had bought second-hand in Aldershot and the only spare room was the dining room, next door to the kitchen. She awoke that night to find the room heaving. Fortunately the cockroaches had the tact to avoid dining-room hours nor had they learned yet to climb the stairs.

Twice a week at lunchtime, while John kept the children, she accompanied a new friend who had been badly injured in a riding accident to the local swimming baths. As the baths were closed to the public during the lunch hour to enable the handicapped to exercise, she and Pauline were often the only swimmers. It was a hateful experience. The schools had been in all morning and the water was filthy, unmentionably so. They stood it because there was no alternative, but Betty herself was seldom to go to any swimming bath ever again. The experience sickened her for life.

Michael, now six, was going regularly to a small private school called St Olave's, which catered especially for musical children. His fees were covered by John who taught music there twice a week. Every morning either she or John took him the perilous journey through the heart of the town and every afternoon met him at 3. 30. He would ride on his tricycle and she would strap Jeremy on to the seat on the back of her bike and they would negotiate the narrow roads together mostly on the pavement where they occasionally sent the pedestrians flying.

The main event of that first year was the Coronation. There were street parties, services and a pageant. Betty Lickiss, a bonny red-haired girl, was to be Good Queen Bess and she chose Michael to be her pageboy. Mrs Hughes kitted him out in ruff, doublet and hose and the Dean loaned him his ceremonial sword. Quite why the pageboy had to have a sword she never did discover but it made Michael's day. No one within two yards of him was safe. Unfortunately it was very wet weather and as his ruff, a paper pie-crust, got soaked, so it drooped lower and lower round his neck until it finally fell off. His hose wrinkled round his ankles but he didn't care. He ran around brandishing his sword, a menace to everyone. For him at least it was a very happy day.

One of his less happy days was the tea party with the Bishop, a kindly if remote and shy bachelor who felt it was his duty to get to know all the clergy in his diocese. While she concentrated on keeping Jeremy, who had just started to walk, away from the shelves of books and other tempting ornaments, and John did his best with small talk, the poor Bishop who was also trying hard, unfortunately managed to scratch Michael's face with his Episcopal ring. There were tears and apologies and a lot of embarrassment all round. Not a good day.

John's three years contract at the cathedral lasted just over two years. Betty's uncle, who was a patron of St Olaf's Episcopal Church, Kirkwall in Orkney, wrote to John offering him the post of rector. That was how things were done in those days. 'Daddy is looking for a minor canon,' took them to Ripon. On this occasion it was Uncle Pat looking for a new rector that took John back to his first love, the Episcopal Church in Scotland and his first and only parish in the Diocese of Aberdeen.

The Bishop of Ripon did not approve. 'It is not in Mr Marshall's interest to leave the Diocese of Ripon,' he wrote to his colleague in Aberdeen. Fortunately 'Plus' Aberdeen did not agree. He was delighted to welcome a Scottish priest back to Scotland. Although they were both sorry in many ways to leave Ripon, this was Orkney, her father's beloved home and John was more than ready for a parish of his own.

Reflections

Cathedral worship is not to everyone's taste. My experience of it during that first year was limited to a handful of Evensongs when John was officiating. I liked what I heard and what I saw, but it felt more like entertainment than worship. I enjoyed singing in the smaller churches especially the *Venite* and the *Te Deum* to familiar tunes. It was not enough for me in those days just to listen, however beautiful the settings.

. With Jeremy to care for and Michael to take to Sunday School, I tended to avoid the cathedral in favour of the two small daughter churches for which John, during that first year at Ripon, was responsible. The congregations were small and old and John wanted to build them up whereas Mr Dean wanted him to encourage their congregations to attend the cathedral. Not exactly kill them off, but certainly not to build them up which may have been the reason why, after a year, he invited John to become the precentor, a post for which with his musical skills he was well able to fulfil. By that time we had both made friends among the elderly pensioners in the almshouses and built up a relationship with those members who had never felt at ease in the formal atmosphere of the cathedral and never would.

I discovered the pleasures of home visiting in those days and would take Jeremy with me as I sat in the neat little homes and listened to life stories some of which were enthralling. We never talked about God but I never doubted his benevolent presence and nor, I think, did they, those fine old men and women in their neat little almshouses.

However even then I was beginning to see that the God of Matins who expected grovelling from 'us miserable sinners who had no health in us' was a lot bigger and greater and kinder than the austere and finger-wagging figure the church occasionally made him out to be. I was not yet mature enough to find him in the psalms but I caught occasional glimpses of him in the collects as the one who was always willing 'to pour upon us the continual dew of thy blessing' and as 'the author of peace and concord' (This was before the days when the word concord' conjured up an image of a gigantic airbus) and as the enlightener of darkness. (I was still mightily afraid of the dark.)

I tried but not hard enough with my prayers. The cathedral loomed over our bedroom and I was very conscious of its protective mass. Occasionally, though, I saw it as menacing, a warning and a threat because I did not really believe that God enjoyed grovelling. My little Centennial Prayer Book with its pages of self-examination made me feel guilty because I was aware that I had committed every one of those sins against God, my neighbour and myself. Did God really care that I had made an 'unworthy communion' or that I concealed 'part of the truth' or looked too long in the mirror. I was fast beginning to turn God into a creation of my own needs. I belittled him for I saw him as I wanted him to be, indulgent, kind and protective, especially of me and my family.

I also realised even then that my role in the church would be with the children. Having not been allowed to attend Sunday School myself I would compensate by teaching Sunday School. Ripon Cathedral had a wonderful afternoon Sunday School with a full complement of teachers under a comfortable and inspiring elderly leader to which I took Michael. I saw the projects, the playlets, the enjoyment on the faces of the children as they tumbled out of the hall clutching pictures, Christmas angels or Easter eggs. Brownies would have to do me for the time being but hopefully one day I would have a Sunday School of my own.

My enrolment in the MU took me to the occasional meeting, but the membership consisted of older, wiser and far more competent women than I could ever hope to be. Instead I was encouraged to join the Young Wives branch of the MU but I attended few meetings. John was out himself most evenings and we could not afford Betty Lickiss' baby-sitting services very often, but I was well aware of how helpful the women's organisations could be to the running of a parish and I learned a lot from my occasional attendances.

I also learned an immense amount from watching Mrs Hughes who became my model parson's wife, unfailingly kind, never too tired to listen, a bit like my own mother who was always so thoughtfully generous. Though I was well aware that I did not have Mrs Hughes' patience, her lack of arrogance and her domestic skills, the main lesson she taught me was that clergy wives have their own ministry. It was not necessarily easy but that it could be a lot of fun if you didn't interfere in the running of the parish and didn't take yourself or your role too seriously.

Chapter Six

Orkney

St Olaf's was an ideal first parish for any priest with a young family. It included all the islands with a smaller church in Stromness, St Mary's, which held an afternoon service every Sunday and a beautiful little chapel at Graemeshall still regularly used. The complex in Kirkwall consisted of the church linked at the vestry end to a fair-sized hall and at the porch end to a fine stone-built, four bed-roomed Rectory. The church's claim to fame was a rood screen which had been filched from St Magnus Cathedral at the time of the Reformation.

Betty's own links with Orkney went back to the 17th century for her direct ancestor had been the first Reformation Bishop of Orkney (who had probably done the filching), one Patrick Graham, a younger son of the Grahams of Inchbrakie, who himself fathered four sons, one of whom remained in Orkney, married locally and was the progenitor of the Graemes of Orkney. The Bishop's bed (remarkably small) was - and still is - to be seen in Skaill House where he had once lived which overlooked the remarkable remains of the Stone Age village of Skara Brae. His direct descendant, the current laird, Patrick Sutherland Graeme, patron of the parish, Lord Lieutenant of Orkney and Betty's uncle, lived at Graemeshall. The chapel had been built by Betty's grandfather for his wife Margaret who had been the youngest daughter of the Revd John Mason Neale. Betty's father, Kenneth (Uncle Pat's younger brother), had preached his first sermon there to his own family. How scary must that have been.

Uncle Pat, a widower, was cared for by his second and unmarried daughter, Alison. Now in her forties, Alison and her great friend Marjorie, daughter of the late J. Storer Clouston, author of the best-seller *A Spy in Black,* were both clever, kind women, experts in bird life of Orkney and leading officials in the Guide movement. They were also pillars of St Olaf.

Somehow the small parish managed to pay their removal fees from Ripon and the redecoration of the Rectory which had been let for some years because the previous Rector, Mr Ward, had been a bachelor and had used part of the church hall for his accommodation. It had been decided to let Betty chose the paper for redecorating. Not really a good idea for her choice was odd to say the least of it. The large sitting room, she decided, should have different papers and contrasting colours, stripes on the long wall and circles on the two shorter walls. To give you an idea of how badly they matched, several people remarked on seeing the end result, 'That's nice, dear,' pointing to the Regency stripes, 'but when is the painter coming to finish the rest of it?' Even to her eyes, the two papers side by side looked a little odd. Worse was the hall and stairwell; she chose black paper with wild flowers sprinkled on it. Bearing in mind the hall and stairs were dark in the first place, the black paper made them dangerously so. For all that, she loved the wild flower motif and no one in the family dared to criticise. Both Alison and Marjorie were remarkably tactful, their only comment being, 'Interesting.' Artistic it was not.

There was no women's group in Orkney, and, though most of the congregation lived outside Kirkwall, there were enough local women to want one. So Betty, fresh from her enrolment into the Mothers Union and her experiences at Ripon, together with John to introduce a spiritual dimension, invited the flower arrangers, cleaners and interested others to tea and discussion in the newly-decorated Rectory. The upshot was the Ladies Fellowship.

'Ladies!' chorused Alison and Marjorie in mock horror. 'You simply can't call it 'Ladies' anything.'

'Why not?' Betty asked, but of course she sort of knew. However it was too late. The newly appointed committee members of the Ladies Fellowship were adamant. They were 'Ladies' not 'Women', so Ladies Fellowship it stayed and it was fun. Fund raising events were planned. Speakers found for fortnightly meetings and 'outings' (frequent outings) arranged.

One of those outings became a talking point in Kirkwall. The organist, Mr G, was the Customs and Excise Officer for the Highland Park Distillery, a lovely man who also ran the local annual operetta performances. Mr G invited the 'ladies' on a personal tour of Highland Park Distillery. A bus picked them all up outside the church at 7.30, drove them to the distillery and handed them over to Mr G at the gates. Her memory of what happened next was a little hazy but a lot of tasting was done and much later the long-suffering bus driver was kind enough to offer his arm to each 'lady' from the bus steps right up to her own front door. The other churches in Kirkwall were duly scandalised.

They were such sports, those 'ladies', game for anything; an open boat trip to Hoy to see the Old Man, a fun day at Graemeshall with flower-pot races, regular Whist Drives and a disastrous Burns Supper. In those days a haggis was not enclosed in plastic as it is today but a frail skin said to be a sheep's bladder. To heat, it required the greatest of care for, if allowed to boil, the skin burst. It was her job to heat seventeen of these small bladders on the Rectory cooker and on pain of death prevent them from boiling. She duly watched while the others set the tables, cooked and mashed potatoes and neeps in the small hall kitchen and the guests began to arrive.

Then the phone went. She ran through to the study to answer. When she came back, the pot was boiling merrily and every one of the haggises had burst. Through the ingenuity of Miss A, a mushy heap was strained and piled onto a serving dish and duly piped in. But it was not the same. There was nothing much to pipe in, still less plunge the knife into, as Burns' Ode to a Haggis required, but, as everyone said, the tatties and neeps were excellent.

Miss A - Meta - was their baby sitter, a little round woman of indeterminate age and engaged to be married. Orkney weddings are notorious for celebration but Meta's was to be very small, about two dozen people in all with a drink and cake at the local hotel afterwards. The service went well, Meta looked nice in a blue two-piece outfit, and, after the service somewhat sedately, they all trooped down Dundas Crescent to the hotel. The waitress came round with a decanter full of a brownish liquid which Betty took to be sherry. (She had smoked and drunk during all of her pregnancies because no one told her not to.) She duly held out her glass. The waitress who knew better shook her head and whispered, 'It'll be lemonade for you.' The liquid was neat whisky. Within ten minutes the atmosphere had changed.

Everyone was laughing or shouting in broad Orcadian and perjink little Meta was sitting on John's knee. It turned out to be a very boozy wedding. The only sober people left in the room were herself and John. When the time came he had to drive the couple to the airport for their honeymoon. Everyone else, especially the bride and groom, was legless.

Alison was born in the local hospital in 1956. There had been a glut of babies that June and the gas-and-air machine had broken down. It was all very painful and in the labour ward she blasphemed rather loudly. The midwife sat across the room and read her Bible and tut-tutted at every, 'Damn-blast-bloody-hell's-teeth and God Almighty.' It could have been a lot worse. The four-letter words beginning with f and s were more or less unknown - at least to Betty - in those days.

Alison looked exactly like her father. The first morning at home, John brought his communicant of the morning (he held a daily Communion service in every parish he served, arranging it so that he had at least one person present as congregation) back to breakfast. Betty came down with Alison in her arms. Miss B stared at her. 'How like her father,' she commented, quickly adding, 'but of course they change.'

Alison did not change. She was a Marshall right from the beginning inheriting her father's humour and his talent for music. The congregation took them all to their heart. She did not have to buy anything for the baby. Everything was provided from carrycot to posh second-hand pram and even a cleaner for a month after the birth. Only a potty was missing.

The congregation consisted of young families like themselves with one or two notable exceptions such as the Professor and his wife. A descendent of William Morris, the Professor Emeritus was a formidable parishioner. He and his wife sat directly behind the Rectory pew. Jeremy, at four years old, spent most of the service under the pew or squatting with his back to the altar. She had no idea what he got up to until he caught bronchitis and was too unwell to go to church. A little gift of honey arrived one morning with a card addressed to 'Jeremy with the "Brown Katy's"'. The only person who has ever dared to be rude to me'. Apparently he spent most of the service staring at the Professor with his tongue stuck out.

The elderly couple decided to ask Betty and John to tea separately, 'so that we can get to know you properly'. A nice idea. A tea party without the children would be a relief. It turned out to be an ordeal. The house was full of priceless ornaments and William Morris memorabilia. She sat there on the edge of her chair and answered the questions fired at her. In desperation she asked would they mind if she smoked. She was granted a grudging permission (most people smoked in those days) but there was no ash-tray. Her ash grew longer and longer. In desperation she asked for help. 'Fetch the old blue chipped saucer, Carl', Mrs Professor demanded of her husband. Betty escaped as soon as possible.

With regard to smoking, she decided the time had come to give up. Although she tried to limit her intake to ten Players Weights (the little ones) a day, the number had crept up to fifteen and was still creeping. She had developed a smoker's cough and it was still too expensive.

She would stop on her thirtieth birthday. That night they returned from holidaying in Fortrose to attend a cocktail party at Eric Linklater's sister's house in Dounby. Uncle Pat, a heavy smoker himself, was there, 'You'll never do it,' he told her complacently and fed her Will's *Goldflake Extra Strong* all evening. Her eyes were running and her throat sore by the time they got home. She never smoked another cigarette, except sometimes in her dreams.

The trouble then was with weight; all those extra sweeties sucked to compensate for nicotine. She would bribe Michael to run to Miss Petrie's wee shop up the hill to buy her wine gums. She would even eat a bar of chocolate while pushing the pram up Dundas Crescent. She ballooned almost over night. It took Teddy Z, the husband of one of her friends, to tell her to lose weight. Teddy was a glamorous Pole who flirted with all the wives. 'You used to be so attractive,' he whispered.in her ear. 'You could be again,' and a lot more fascinating flannel. Whatever it was, it worked. She began to diet. That was the beginning of a long see-saw battle with weight. She tried all the new fads from counting calories to the grapefruit diet. They only worked for a while.

She began to write seriously again. A visit from John Betjeman one Sunday inspired her. He was on a National Trust cruise and had taken time off to visit St Olaf's for the morning service. John Betjeman was one of those few people who have true charisma. Once met they are never forgotten. The fact that he had liked the church, complimented John's sermon and taken the time to come into the Rectory for a brief cup of coffee before returning to his ship was an experience she was never to forget.

Eric Linklater's mother, a sprightly nonogenarian, the daughter of a sea captain, who herself had sailed before the mast and had written a book about her experiences, also inspired her, as did the great Eric himself. He came north from time to time to see his mother and his sister and Betty was always tongue-tied with shyness in the presence of a real writer. However, after a drink or two at a cocktail party, she found herself in the great man's presence and asked him about his latest book. For the next blissful half hour he told her the plot of *The Simmer Dim*. What she did not realise then was just how much some writers like to be asked about their books. She was to be one of them. Years later, a member of the current congregation sidled up to her one Sunday after church during coffee in the hall and whispered, 'I enjoyed your book, dearie, but I didn't want to say anything, in case you wouldn't like it.' As if it was some sort of dirty secret. No one else in that congregation ever said anything. It was obvious that Eric Linklater enjoyed talking at length about his books. It transpired that John had baptised one of his children in Old St Pauls so there was plenty to talk about. She did not quite like to tell him about her own writing.

She had begun another novel, a huge piece of work which coincidentally followed the story line of Mary MacCarthy's *Reunion*, (though there the resemblance ended). Hers too was about a reunion after ten years of five girls who had been close friends at boarding school. It followed in detail their separate and diverse lives up to that point and it was very long. She called it *Quintessence* and sent it off to a publisher who was looking for new writers. She actually got a letter back. 'This is a formidable length for a first novel,' the editor had written. 'Send us your next.'

Rejection slips have their own hierarchy. Those with a scribbled note were to be preferred to the bare printed sheet, whereas a proper letter was just a whisker away from acceptance. First novels are usually autobiographical. *Quintessence* was five aspects of herself, she realised later. She sent it to several other publishers and then put it aside for good. By that time she was well into another book. This was the secret, she discovered, to be well into another book while the rejection slips for the previous one piled up. That way they didn't hurt so much. The next book would be better.

Her love-hate relationship with the Royal Mail started at that time. She learned to distinguish by the drop of the post through the letterbox the sound of success or failure. Failure equalled the depressing thump of a returned manuscript. There were to be a lot of thumps over the next decade She took a long time to learn her craft. Meanwhile she was writing short stories, articles and Sunday School plays.

Congregations tend to reflect the age of the Rectory family, or so she was to discover over the years. In Kirkwall the majority of members were young married couples with children under ten and they all came to Sunday School. Now was her chance to enjoy what she herself had never been allowed to experience as a child. She was given a sum of money by the church treasurer to spend on equipment and poured over catalogues for work books, and Bible story stamps with neat little folding cards, and soon she had her Sunday School off the mark. Afternoon classes had by that time given way to Sunday morning sessions in the hall with the children attending the first part of Matins which would include a children's hymn and then trooping off to the adjacent hall where their parents picked them up after the service.

The secret of a successful Sunday School was always to have a project on hand. The Christmas Nativity play occupied most of the autumn session, the Spring term included a Lent Sunday soup and pudding lunch made by mums for the congregation but served by the children in the hall, and the Easter Garden, while in the summer term the children had a stall at the garden fete to prepare for and the 'picnic' to look forward to.

Small disasters happened from time to time like the angry mum who rang up one Sunday afternoon to complain that she had not sent her son to Sunday School to learn how to swear. (The word was 'bugger'). Betty knew exactly who the culprit was, an angelic little boy, who was not to blame. He just copied his father.

Sunday School picnics in Orkney ranged from one part of the islands to another but always included a beach, three-legged races, sand castle competitions, treasure hunts and of course bottles of 'ginger' - gaudily coloured, flavoured soda water - to go with the lashings of food provided by the parents. These picnics were soon to become parish outings.

The date of the Nativity Play was always a small bone of contention between her and John. The play, like the carol service, was traditionally put on after Christmas, not a popular date with the children or the parents, still less with her. But when she suggested the Sunday before Christmas, John dug his heels in. You did not, in those days, 'anticipate' Christmas. It was still Advent right up to Christmas Eve. Thus no plays, no carol services were allowed until after the great day by which time, the children had lost their zeal. One year a compromise was made for Christmas afternoon, but that was still more unpopular. A following year it was Christmas morning during the service but she realised that was not really fair on her own children, whose Christmases were disrupted enough already. It took many years for John to allow her to stage the play before Christmas, but it worked so much better that way.

Another bone of contention was the use of chasubles for the three Wise Men. These were not church robes but had belonged to her father and one, very ornate and pink, to her great-grandfather. The little boys looked so good in them, especially Michael, that she was devastated when John put his foot down. He was quite right of course and deep down she knew it. These were garments used by priests at the altar. In the end they had to make use of tablecloths and cut-down old evening dresses.

Christmas days in St Olaf's were hectic. Gifts rolled in including one turkey and two geese from farming members of the congregation, feathers and guts still intact. How to dispose of them? There were no freezers in those days. They decided to invite two Shetland Episcopalian families who lived on the other side of the mainland for Christmas lunch and anyone else who happened to be alone, in all some thirty people counting themselves and including some ten children. They would serve the meal in the adjacent church hall. Disembowelling the birds and removing the tendons from the legs took hours. In the end John pulled one end of the goose and she the other. They were tough old birds. Everything that could be done beforehand like the chestnut stuffing, the brandy butter and the fruit salad was finished. All that had to be done on the morning (all) was roast the birds and tatties, heat the peas (ten tins of them) and steam the two large puds she had made in time for 'stir-up' Sunday (so called from the prayer book collect for the Sunday next before Advent.)

A minibus was duly hired for the visitors, two long trestle tables set with sheets for tablecloths, the gramophone wound up, crackers and sweets provided. What could go wrong?

Leaving everything either in the Rectory oven or in the electric cooker in the hall she went off to church with the children as high as kites. As soon as the service was done she rushed over to the hall to see to the roasting tatties and steaming puds and there was Mr G, the organist, about to swallow a Christmas dram from a flask in his pocket.

'You'll not refuse to drink a toast with me on Christmas morning,' he said, reaching for a teacup and pouring out the remains of his flask, which amounted to three quarters of the cup. There was no time to argue. She quaffed back the brown stuff in one long spluttering gulp.

Quite how the lunch progressed she could not afterwards remember. Somehow it all happened and everyone was fed. Afterwards when she got back to the Rectory she found that ten tins of processed peas had simmered themselves dry. They made rather a good soup.

Orcadians were incredibly generous. No week went by without the gift of a pair of rabbits, a hare or half a dozen small, delicious sea trout and/or a boiling fowl. She became quite skilled at skinning rabbits, gutting fish and plucking hens under her cousin Alison's tutelage. No squeamishness allowed. Hares seemed to have a lot more blood in them than rabbits. Why was that? But she managed jugged hare too. During the season, the manager of a lobster fishing industry, a church member, brought her a pair of live creatures every week. Much as she liked to eat lobster herself, the children hated it and John only ate it because it was there. Every time she plunged them into boiling water, she tried to convince herself that the ensuing scream was just escaping air. In the end she could stand it no longer and had to decline that particular gift.

Then there was the winter of the great freeze. Orkney did not usually have snow for more than a day or two each winter so when it started in January and lasted into March they made the most of it. Clay Loan was a long steep hill that led down to the main street. Closed to traffic for most of that winter, weekend mornings and every afternoon were for the children to go sledging and in the evenings the mums and dads came out. Small children in those days went to bed at about seven after which the adults were free to take over their sledges and enjoy themselves in the snow under street lights. It was the same at the tennis courts in the summer. The children were encouraged to play in the daytime and then at night the adults came out. Midnight tennis on the longest day in June when it never got really dark was strictly for grown-ups. Teddy Z was much the best player and when she and her partner managed to win one game in a set against him it was a matter of huge pride. She spent a lot of afternoons on the tennis courts while the pre-school children played happily together in a small area beside the pavilion.

Snow might have been a rare treat but gales were frequent. Once in a particularly bad one she took the boys down to the harbour to see the water. It was a terrifying and stupid thing to do. Metal dustbin lids narrowly missed them as they bowled through the streets. Though the sea seemed to have turned to smoke, spume

88

spat at them and soaked them to the skin. The two boys dangled at the end of her hands as the wind lifted them off their feet. No wonder Orkney had so few trees. Next time they would all stay safely indoors.

Because the weather was so variable, a day that combined sun and warmth and was wind-free was a rare event, especially a day towards the end of June which seemed to go on for ever. Then Orkney became the most beautiful place in the world.

In September rehearsals for Mr G's annual operetta began. For years the choice had been Gilbert and Sullivan but he wanted to try something different. *Pink Champagne* was his first option, a version of *Die Fledermaus* for amateurs and he asked if Betty would like to join the chorus. She certainly would. It was a massive undertaking for Mr G with the orchestra to rehearse as well as the soloists and the chorus to coach. The following year a Dvorak operetta was chosen based on his *New World Symphony* followed by a life of Greig. Then she was pregnant and that was the end of operettas for her. Cultural life in Orkney was diverse and intense. She particularly enjoyed the Literary Society though there was one extremely embarrassing moment. The speaker for that evening had chosen to talk about Yeats. Unfortunately the erudite English teacher asked to introduce him had not been briefed properly, either that or he was slightly the worse for drink, because he gave a neat little summary of the work of Keats.

The year after the fiasco of the Burns Supper in the Church Hall she was invited by the Chamber of Commerce to give the reply to the Toast to the Lassies at their grand Burns Supper in the Town Hall. The Revd Mr Chirgwin, a scholar and Church of Scotland minister was to give the toast to the Immortal Memory and the various other speakers were all equally competent. Betty was terrified, so scared that she consulted Dr Jimmy who prescribed the same pills as he gave to the local football team before a match to calm their nerves. She was to take them regularly for three days before and ease off slowly over three days afterwards but she was on no account to drink any alcohol. A Burns Supper without alcohol? She listened as the speeches droned on, every one a little longer than the last, while the laughter grew ever more raucous. By the time it came to her turn to speak she could have recited the twice times table and it would have made no difference. Everyone was drunk, herself (and John) excepted.

Another cringe-making evening occurred when her cousin Alison invited them both to provide an evening's entertainment for her local SWRI (Scottish Women's Rural Institute) in St Mary's Holm. Easy for John. He just had to sit down at the piano and play. This he did and he also elected to read James Thurber's short story. *The Night the Bed fell on Father.* He read it well and everyone dutifully laughed. Then it was her turn. What could she do? These women were all farmers' wives, country-women and one of the many things they did superbly well was cook. Considering her audience, Betty's choice of entertainment was startling. A recipe for Butterscotch Trifle. 'Take one jam Swiss roll (bought) one tin of peaches, one tin of Nestles cream, one packet of Butterscotch Angel Delight mixed with one pint of milk and one small glass of sherry...' Yes, well, Betty thought it was good and John and the children had never complained!

Michael and Jeremy settled into Kirkwall Grammar School and made friends. One boy, Nixon by name, a near neighbour, was particularly athletic. On the School Sports day, whenever he appeared, a shout echoed round the field, 'up' with whoever it might be, and, invariably 'down with knickers'. Michael and Jeremy creased up with laughter. John had a fairly devastating experience at Kirkie Grammar. Asked to take some music lessons during the illness of the relevant teacher he found himself at the centre of a tiered classroom filled with large and somewhat lumpen teenage girls. In those days, the classroom was heated by a coal fire. He made the mistake of asking for a volunteer to put on more coal. Immediately there was an almighty crash as all thirty girls stampeded down to answer his request. He emerged from that lesson white and shaking and not a little wiser.

Most days they entertained or were invited out. Twice or three times a week they had regular lunch visitors. Iain, a doctor from Shapinsay who visited his hospital patients came every Tuesday. They had lengthy un-rancorous political arguments which Betty much enjoyed. Mike came on Thursdays. He worked part time for his uncle in Kirkwall and also ran a farm. He and his wife were perhaps her closest friends. Then there was Lance who worked for a seaweed company and whose baby John baptised. On Sunday evenings they seldom went out but looked forward to a visit from the local minister and his wife. All of them, exhausted after the rigours of Sunday, usually fell about laughing over something as silly as the notorious Du St Bin who was due to be removed on Monday morning or was it Tuesday?

On evenings out to supper, rather than pay for baby sitters, they bundled the children into the back of the Morris Minor and put them to bed in their hosts' houses. John's only stipulation was no engagements on Saturday evenings. He liked to be well prepared for Sundays which included two morning services in St Olafs, a service in St Marys, Stromness, at 3 pm and back again to St Olafs for Evensong. While John officiated in Stromness she took the children to the nearest beach. Ah those beaches.... Scapa was closest and they spent a lot of time there. Waulkmill Bay was perhaps best. When the tide was in you could walk for miles in shallow water. Betty's mother agonised over Michael who fearlessly almost disappeared from view as he wandered out to sea, the water no higher than his knees. Her favourite place was Deerness where there were puffins. Once Alison was old enough to go on the back of her bike, they would all set out for long bike rides between great banks of pink clover and golden buttercups. Orkney wild flowers seemed to have a deeper hue than their Scottish counterparts, including the adorable little *Primula Scotica*

All that was Orkney from Scara Brae to Maeshow, from St Magnus Cathedral to the little chapel of St Margaret at Graemeshall and the Italian Chapel on Langholm, from the towering and dangerous bird-limed cliffs of Yesnaby to the Viking remains on Birsay, not forgetting the families of St Olaf and St Mary, was theirs for six glorious years.

When John came to her one day with a letter inviting him to consider becoming Rector of St Peter's, Galashiels, she did not think to argue him out of it. He believed he had been called but it was a heart-breaking move for all of them. She spent their leaving party shut up in the little vestry because she could not stop crying. All her friends visited her there and cried too.

Reflections

I took my Sunday School work seriously. When the vestry of St Olafs, at John's suggestion, offered to pay my expenses to attend a Sunday School Teachers Training Week at Walkerburn in Peebleshire, I was excited about attending. I don't know what I expected but it turned out to be enormous fun. Although most of the others on the course were still teenagers, there were also two young priests and we three spent a lot of the time walking in the Border hills, lingering over meals and laughing.

The Adviser of Sunday Schools in the SEC and our tutor for the week was Miss Margaret Marshall, a stout, short and rather scary middle-aged woman who became our friend for life. She knew every church and all the rectors including their families probably better than anyone else in the Province for she spent her days driving in her familiar Morris Minor from parish to parish, weekending in draughty rectories to observe Sunday Schools, train teachers and the clergy, and she undoubtedly had her favourites. It was not a good idea to fall foul of Miss Marshall. She was also a lifeline. The clergy, unless they worked in the cities or had attended college together, tended not to know each other that well and the link between neighbouring parishes was often non-existent. If you wanted to know whose children were doing what, whose congregations were booming (not many), who was tipped to be a canon, or even a bishop, Miss Marshall knew and she would pass on the information if you were one of the favoured few. We never quite knew where we were in the pecking order of favourites but we always enjoyed her visits.

Who was it who said that 'the spiritual health of a nation may be judged by the number and strength of its religious', here meaning its monks and nuns. In the first half of the nineteenth century the SEC had representatives from many of the Anglican orders in all the major cities. First had been in 1862 when a Sister from the

Society St Margaret's Convent in East Grinstead founded by my great-grandfather had come to Aberdeen. Those coming later included a handful of Sisters of the Society of St Peter the Apostle from their mother house in Laleham Abbey who had come north in 1919 to do community work first in Joppa and then in Perth. Finally in 1935 they had acquired the large house and grounds of Sunnybrae in Walkerburn by Innerleithen in Peebleshire and later added the adjacent mansion of Stoneyhill. For some forty years these few and ageing sisters organised private and conducted Retreats and held conferences and training sessions throughout the year.

I fell in love with Walkerburn, the walled gardens sheltered by those great round rolling Border hills and those tall green trees, such a contrast to the flat and treeless landscape of Orkney. The rooms were spacious, flower-filled and the food superb. I remember one day opening by mistake a wrong door at the top of the stairs. It was only a cupboard, tiny, windowless, and it was entirely filled by a small bed. This was one of the Sister's cells. It was a sad day for the SEC when the two houses had to be closed. Those lovely, tireless Sisters had finally grown too old, there had been too few novices and there was no money anyhow.

Much as I hated leaving Orkney, the thought that Galashiels was so close to Walkerburn was like a small candle in the gloom, as indeed it proved to be.

Looking back on our time in Orkney I see it as one long happy holiday under massive skies which were more often grey than blue but always beautiful. And God? I saw him as a comfortable Matinsy sort of Dad who loved us all in a comfortable Dadsy sort of way and who had set our paths in the pleasantest of places. Our three children were a joy, we had good friends in and out of the parish and loving relatives. I would have been happy to spend the rest of my life in Orkney

Chapter Seven

Galashiels

From a whole house in Kirkwall they moved into a rectory that was only half a house in Galashiels. It had been divided by a previous incumbent who had had no family and it was never quite big enough for them. The drawing room was spacious and cold, the dining room adequate as was John's study, but the kitchen was minute and there were only two large bedrooms and one tiny room. The boys had to share and when their cousin, Kenneth, came for the school holidays (Bunty and Peter and their younger children were living in Ceylon) that end room became a dormitory.

The other half of the house was owned by a friendly old couple called Baird. He was a retired postmaster, they had no family and could probably have managed with less room. They had a small and carefully tended garden. The Rectory nine-tenths was an enormous wilderness. So large, in fact, that it contained a bungalow with its own garden which housed a retired head teacher from St Peter's local Episcopal Primary School. At one time, church, school, rectory and graveyard were all part of the same complex. Only a small part of the grounds had been portioned off to accommodate the Bairds and Miss Thompson. The old school building now housed the current head master and his German wife, Clara. The school itself had been enlarged and rebuilt outside the grounds across the lane. The verger and family lived in part of the vast church hall and he tended the church lawns and graveyard. The rest of the grounds which included an orchard of ageing apple trees, a tar-macadam drive with its accompanying shrubbery, a giant Wellingtonia, a vast yew hedge, spectacular in misty weather for it was shrouded in cobwebs, and enough space to run a market garden.

Under Mr Baird's watchful and encouraging eye and thanks to his generous sharing of his herbaceous plants she was encouraged to turn it back into the garden it had obviously once been. She could expect no help from John. His was a large parish, he had no car and he spent his mornings after daily mass and a weekly school assembly on his sermons, office and paperwork, his afternoons visiting hospitals and parishioners and his evenings at meetings or organisations. Eventually he bought a second-hand scooter, but he was so unsafe that he was stopped several times by the police for going too slowly! He had other difficulties too for they were a nit-picking vestry quick to report any perceived demeanour to the bishop. The first of these occurred within their first fortnight. He moved the lectern precisely a foot forwards to give the readers enough room to stand behind it without having to go into the chancel Sacrilege. The bishop rang him to advise him to go slow with any changes he might want to make. These were Border folk.

The other booboo was his grateful acceptance of the gift of a crimson aisle carpet to replace the coconut matting from the powerful Mothers Union without first consulting the vestry. He also fell foul of the organist who was accustomed to choosing the hymns without consultation. There were the usual problems with churchmanship. He was not 'high' enough for some, and 'next door to Rome' to others. Not a hope here of a mid-morning Sunday Eucharist which he aspired to hold in all his parishes. It was Matins, shortened once a month to accommodate a late Communion service for which only a handful remained.

That first year 'Stewardship' was the word on every Episcopal tongue. The Commission appointed by the SEC recommended 'a truly general and very carefully organised effort' to convince congregations that giving to the work of the church was a duty not an option. By employing professional fund-raisers, some churches were finding that Stewardship Campaigns, though frighteningly expensive, were doing wonders for church finances elsewhere, so St Peters vestry decided to try one. A limited company in the visible form of a pretty girl with a telephone was installed in one of the smaller rooms adjoining the church hall. Quite what she did, Betty never fully understood, but she drank pints of coffee in the Rectory, talked a lot about her cousin the film star, Oliver Reed, and telephoned her family who lived in Australia rather too frequently. Nevertheless, a glossy brochure was produced, a dinner organised in the town hall and every member of the congregation asked to pledge a weekly regular sum of money in exchange for small envelopes to contain it. A lot of people grumbled at the expense, that the church was always after money and forgot that the true message was about more than money. Stewardship of Time, Talents and Tithes, was the motto. Tithes came third on the list but that was the only one folk remembered. Promises were made that the congregation would never be asked for another penny, no more jumble sales, summer fetes or fund-raising events. Perhaps for a year that promise was kept. Thereafter the calendar was as full as ever it had been of jumble sales, whist drives and daffodil teas. The Stewardship Fund-raisers had forgotten that sales and beetle-drives and Bingo nights are the life-blood of any congregation, occasions for fellowship and fun (well sometimes). It all worked for a while but as the cost of living rose the only thing that did not go up was church giving so that after a few years church finances were more or less back to square one.

But these were only pinpricks. The congregation was hard working, conscientious, generous, mainly working class and many of them connected in some way with the mills. Three county families attended, kind, supportive people who descended from a great height, but the majority of wealthy folk including the farmers went to the Episcopal church in Melrose. St Peters operated on a shoe-string.

Betty had never been so busy in her life. The garden took over a lot of her time. She was writing regularly and there were Mothers Union meetings, Sunday School classes and shows to prepare for, not to mention her own children.

Thanks to her mother's generosity the boys attended a small preparatory school in Melrose. There was a good reason for this. She and John hoped that they would get bursaries available for the sons of the clergy at Glenalmond, an Episcopalian public school in Perthshire which provided what were known as 'fil. clers' which paid the full fees for the sons of Episcopalian priests as long as they passed their Common Entrance exam. To work for this they needed the sort of education taught in fee-paying preparatory schools. St Mary's in Melrose provided this, so off they went by bus or bicycle every morning and returned at about five every evening. There was another reason why Betty in particular wanted them to go to St Marys. A close school friend had been the daughter of a previous headmaster and she herself had stayed in one of the dormitories during a summer holiday and had a fondness for the place. The boys didn't like it much but it fulfilled its purpose. Both of them achieved 'fil. clers' and at the age of thirteen joined Glenalmond in Perthshire as boarders.

Alison meanwhile remained at home, until, at the age of five she attended St Peter's Primary School across leafy Parsonage Lane. From time to time she would be invited on her own to have tea with Miss T, the retired headmistress of St Peter's Episcopal School whose bungalow had been built in the Rectory grounds. Miss T was large, exceedingly devout, kind and clever, one of the daily Mass attenders. She had a great nephew, Mikey, who occasionally visited; once memorably on his own with Alison. About the same age, they were left in the kitchen together with paper and crayons the better to get to know each other. Miss T meanwhile went into the sitting room to read her paper. After a short while Alison opened the door. 'Please Miss T,' she said, 'Mikey - '. She got no further. 'I don't want to hear it, Alison. Go back and play.' Seconds later, Alison appeared at the door again. 'Please Miss T, Mik - ' Again she was stopped. 'I told you, Alison, I don't like little girls who tell tales.' Again moments later Alison dared to go back. 'Please, Miss T,' she implored her,' Please come.' Huffing a bit Miss T got up and stalked into the kitchen. 'What's all this about?' she asked crossly. It was only too obvious. The kitchen floor was flooded. Mikey had turned on both taps and was thoroughly enjoying himself splashing about in the water. Miss T never tired of telling the story against herself.

The garden gradually took shape. She dug, she weeded and she planted for about two hours every afternoon. When the boys were on holiday they were roped in to climb the garden wall into the adjacent field which had horses and scoop up the droppings for manure. She had her successes – a hedge of amazingly prolific sweet peas – and her failures - a row of cauliflowers which she was nurturing got cabbage root fly and all died over night. - and a greenhouse full of tomatoes which never ripened.

Writing happened early in the morning. Her mother, bless her, paid for her to take a course in short story writing with the London School of Journalism. It cost £20 pounds for ten lessons, an unthinkable sum to afford for herself, so she scrupulously performed the exercises for a joky tutor whom she got to like on paper and who was encouraging. (Years later when she became a published novelist she arranged to meet him on a visit to London. It was a huge disappointment to them both.) The result of the course was her first publication. The editor of the Scots Magazine wrote to her accepting the first story she had worked on with her tutor. She carried the letter inside her bra for days. In the same week she also had a Nativity play accepted by the Sunday School Chronicle. There it was all written out on the first page of the broadsheet newspaper. Naively she thought that now she had broken into the world of publication, everything she wrote thereafter would be published. Ha!

Meanwhile she was on to her third and fourth novels, one about the election of a bishop in the Episcopal Church, the other a thriller romance set in a country house in the Ochils. She had an audience of a sort. Once a week she met Mrs Baird and Clara Shiach from the schoolhouse for morning coffee in each other's houses and she read the latest chapter. They provided all the encouragement she needed to go on. Not a shadow of boredom crossed their faces as she launched into the latest chapter. How kind was that. Even so, the rejection slips mounted.

The Mothers Union met once a fortnight. As was the custom for the rector's wife, she was soon made the Enrolling Member but by now her disenchantment had taken root. The wife of the verger wanted to join. She had been divorced, but she was a mother, a good and loyal member of St Peters, a tireless cleaner and a constant support. Although the rules about divorcees were still fairly strict in the SEC, John had (after private consultation with the Bishop) admitted her to Communion so Betty had her enrolled. Everyone knew but no one objected. She was after all a mother and there were several members who had no children. In her own eyes she had done no wrong. No one else, thank the Lord, was prepared to cast a stone.

There was also the CWMA (Christian Woman's Missionary Association) which she did not have to organise. That was done by Mrs Hope, an elderly long-time member of the congregation who took her responsibilities with due seriousness. Sales for African babies were arranged, parcels of blankets or children's clothing sent off to the depot in Edinburgh and twice a year subscriptions and other dues squeezed out of everyone. There were at one time 75 members on the role so it kept Mrs Hope busy. By the time John was appointed Rector she was getting old but her zeal never lessened. Betty made a point of visiting her for a cup of tea every Sunday afternoon when she would talk about the glories of St Peters and the saintliness of past rectors in the good old days. (This is something rectors and their wives have to get used to - the splendours of the past, packed congregations and saint-like priests.)

Though the CWMA and the MU were rivals in many ways, most women belonged to both and everyone went on all the outings. These were long arduous days bent on pleasure, spent on buses with high tea at a posh restaurant or hotel often on the other side of the country or even across the Border 'down' to England. The women wore their best clothes, spent hard-earned savings at gift shops and formed little groups at the various bars. Always these outings included a trip to the bar. One year on a long drive up to Pitlochry she was offered a drink by each of the small factions. She slept all the way home.

Sometimes the MU played host to other MUs and laid on splendid teas. One unforgettable Saturday the Bishop's wife (Mrs Warner at the time), came to address the assembled crowd. The noise from the adjoining kitchen grew embarrassing. At the first opportunity, a coffee break, she went over to remonstrate with the group preparing lunch in the kitchen. 'Could you keep the noise level down a little. The Bishop's wife has a very soft voice.'

True, but unfortunately the Bishop's wife was standing behind her at the time. She pretended not to have overheard. What a nice woman. The Bishop was nice too. He was a member of the Edinburgh Zoo committee and together they invited all the clergy wives in the diocese for a day out at the zoo with lunch thrown in.

It was the first and only time she ever met most of them. Some, she noticed - especially the Rector of Kelso's wife - were as smart as paint. 'Everything home-made,' she told Betty with justifiable pride, who felt a bit of a frump beside her.

But it was with the youth of the parish that she spent most of her time. She had soon noticed that when the young people turned twelve or thirteen, they left Sunday School for Confirmation classes with the Rector and after the heady annual Service of Confirmation, the girls in white veils and the boys in shirts and ties, they were seen no more in church. It was almost as if Confirmation was the end of the line, not the beginning of church life. At least it was for the girls. The lads had the Boys Brigade to join which was particularly strong in St Peters with its own services and church parades. Her Sunday School class was a large close group that first year, so they decided to stay together and form a Youth Club to be joined immediately after Confirmation.

The secret of a successful Sunday School or Youth Club which she had learned from Margaret Marshall, was always to have a project in mind. It might be a Talent Show or a Concert. Everyone wanted to take part but unfortunately no one had much talent. The most popular act was to mime a pop song. *Bobby's Girl* was high on the list and there were funny sketches, mostly inaudible, a small pop group consisting of drummer and a couple of learner guitars, a bit of Highland dancing, a recorder or two playing the *Skye Boat Song* or *The Bonnie Banks of Loch Lomond* and a lot of jive dancing. The money raised was partly for themselves in order either to decorate the small hall in Beatles wall-paper or to pay for a bus outing but always a significant percentage went to the church. After one of these shows which had gone without too many hitches and drawn a good house mainly of parents and siblings, she overheard one woman saying to another, 'If it had nae been for a guid cause, I'd have demanded ma money back.' Oh dear, had it really been that bad? Probably.

There were numerous outings. A visit to the TV studios in Glasgow to take part in the *One O'clock Gang Show* hosted by the comedian, Larry Marshall, also included a visit to the cathedral because Betty felt God had to come into it somewhere.

100

It was one of the hottest days of the year and as they padded along the road to St Mary's their stiletto heels stuck in the melting tar. Someone had brought along some foot powder (why, she never found out) and once in the cool of the cathedral they took off their shoes and dusted their swollen feet liberally before going outside to pose in front of the Calvary by the main door to take photos of each other under 'yon fancy Cross'. She hadn't the heart to tell them this was the usual repository for scattering the ashes of the departed.

Few of them had ever visited a city and Betty thought they would enjoy one of the big department stores. They did, but it was the elevators they liked best. 'Gaud ma belly,' said Cathie, as, for the unpteenth time she soared up to the top floor and down again sandwiched between the fur coats and designer shopping bags of an alien species. They all bought presents for their mums in the shape of tea towels or dish mops.

A visit to Princes Street in Edinburgh was nearly a disaster. She could not bring herself to follow their eager climb up the Sir Walter Scott monument and hid her head in terror as they leaned down from that great height and shouted at the tops of their voices, 'Mrs M! Mrs M, look at me!'

Walking through the crowded Princes Street Gardens her noisy group was confronted by a gang of local youths who shoved Jean provocatively, or so she said. It may have been the other way round. Jean was not the best person to shove. She had a quicksilver temper. Both groups squared up for a fight. A policeman was eyeing them. She pushed Jean over to Margaret, her adult assistant, 'Meet you in the Monseigneur,' she muttered. Margaret had the presence of mind to march Jean off briskly in one direction, while she led the others away as fast she could towards the News Theatre across the busy road. Eventually tempers cooled down and in due course they all met up for high tea at the Balmoral restaurant. The journey home by minibus was not without its hazards for every time anyone in trousers, teenager or grandpa, was spotted, they would lean their heads out of the windows and sing at the tops of their voices *Braw Braw lads of Gala Water*, the Galashiels theme song of all time.

A weekend visit to the SEC youth centre at Dalmahoy had its own small crisis. Margaret managed to get locked in the loo on Sunday morning. She was hysterical so Betty had to fetch the Rector, already robed and prepared to take the 8 am communion service in the adjoining chapel. In the end he had to take an axe to the recalcitrant door. A priest robed up with an axe in his hand was an unforgettable experience and not just for the girls.

For one of their many outings they decided to tackle the Three Brethren, a long and sometimes tough climb which would take them over the hills to join the main road where they could catch a bus home. 'Sand-shoes everyone,' Betty pleaded (this was before the days of trainers) but only one had listened, the rest came in their little heeled pumps which made the walk nearly impossible. Better in bare feet. Bless them, no one reneged on the walk. Packed lunches were eaten long before lunchtime but every one of them finished the climb.

Betty thought that they ought at least to be given the chance to learn ball-room dancing so she engaged a local gentleman who arrived in tuxedo, white tie and tails. For that first session, the hall was crowded as boys and girls were instructed in the mysteries of the quick foxtrot. No one said much afterwards but the following week the group was decimated, not a single boy, and only half-a-dozen girls. On disco nights, however, there were at least a hundred kids in the big hall, boys on one side, girls on the other, eyeing each other up, prickly as thistles. On one occasion the verger came in to tell her he had caught two lads running round the graveyard one with a knife in his hand.

Did they ever go to church? Yes indeed. As the girls grew older they became Sunday School assistants sharing out the little ones between them. She was touched one day to watch a communion service with the babies re-enacted by Peggy who had brought lemonade and Smarties for the occasion. In Lent, John held a mid-week evening service. In exchange for their attendance, they came up to the Rectory afterwards to drink ginger and biscuits and watch a particularly gruesome hospital operation programme on telly. A little bribery never came amiss. Soon they were having stalls of their own at the Summer or Christmas Fayres. She grew to love those girls. Do they still attend church? Hopefully some do. One, fifty years later, is a pillar of the local and national Congregational church.

John had Mondays off. He had a long lie and they usually managed to do something together while the children were at school, a trip to Edinburgh, only an hour by train before Beeching closed it down, or a café lunch in town. On Monday nights when John was in to baby-sit, she went on her own to the cinema, no matter what was on. She bought a bar of chocolate, ate it and promptly fell asleep partly from the soporific effects of the chocolate, and partly from sheer exhaustion. If the film was a horror movie she dreaded the walk back in the dark through the graveyard to the Rectory. She would take it at a run and hurl herself through the back door as if all the demons in hell were at her heels. In *Psycho* she actually screamed out aloud.

Christmases were even more fraught than in Orkney without the perks. If her mother was there all went well, otherwise it was a mad scramble throughout December with rehearsals for the Nativity play, church decorating, a rush of parties and the Christmas tree, presents, cards and of course the all-important food. The chestnut stuffing was the hardest. They all loved it so that meant scoring and par-boiling 3 lbs of chestnuts, then the peeling. At least half of them were mouldy and had to be thrown out. The rest were resistant to peeling down to the last shred of under-skin (anyone who had peeled chestnuts will known exactly what this entails) then they had to be boiled again till soft and mashed with all the right ingredients to make them into stuffing. It was a long cumbersome job. She usually made the brandy butter a few days in advance too, and peeled the potatoes the night before. The Christmas Eve service though starting at 11.30 often lingered on till 1 am. She would escape from the good wishes of the packed congregation as soon as possible, rush up to the Rectory to fill stockings and hope the children were asleep or at least pretending to be.

John always put on an 8 am Communion on Christmas morning for there were some who disliked and disapproved of the Midnight Mass so the alarm had to be set for 7. Not that an alarm was

103

needed. The children were usually awake by 5, and not long after bounced through to their bedroom, high as kites. She would drag herself from sleep and remember the turkey had to be in the oven by 9 at the latest.

Apart from the stockings, no presents were opened in the morning which was a hectic rush to get the table set, the turkey in the oven, and the pudding, which she had made weeks before, on the steam. Then down to church for the 11 am service which was mainly attended by young families unable to go out at midnight, a lovely service where the children paraded their presents and everyone sang *Away in a Manager.* She tried to think the right thoughts but her mind could not help fixating on the turkey and roast potatoes left to their own devices in the oven and whether she had remembered to top up the water in the pan that was steaming the pudding

Lunch should have been to die for, all her favourite food with coffee and one of the many gifts of divine chocolates to follow. Three years running, however, she managed to catch a cold which would be just at its worst on Christmas Day so that the food had no taste and she was feeling lousy. Nevertheless presents were duly opened, wrapping paper folded away for the following years, the thank-you list taken, and then, at John's insistence, the whole family trooped about a mile up the road to visit the old folks home where he played the piano for more carols.

On New Year's Day, they went as a family to the Convent Christmas Party at Walkerburn. The bus journey from Galashiels to Innerleithen was hazardous for it was always full of drunk or hung-over men determined to be friendly. She and the boys cowered, John stared out of the window but Alison played up to them and enjoyed their banter for it resulted in handfuls of sixpences and even the odd shilling which the boys, glum and embarrassed, would have liked too. The tea party at Walkerburn included little gifts for everyone of a holy card and ended up with carols round the tree in their spacious entrance hall. Alison, as the youngest, was always asked to sing a solo. Invariably she chose *God rest ye, merry gentlemen*, which Betty had not thought suitable at all.

It was at about this time that something sad happened to Evensong. It had always been a fairly popular service but everywhere numbers were declining. It was said somewhat glibly that the reason was the Sunday evening television showing of *The Forsyte Saga*. And yes, that was why she found herself dodging the evening service more and more often with the lamest of excuses. Like everyone else she was hooked on *The Forsyte Saga*. TV series don't last forever but the numbers did not bounce up again. In fact it was not just Evensong. Between 1940 and 1960 membership of the SEC declined from 115,568 to 97,038 and over the next twenty years by a further 25,000 and not only in Scotland. The church of England were to lose two million members between the '30s and the '90's, a decrease of 60%.

After a couple of years, John's father, now back from Australia settled with his mother in West Kilbride, got bowel cancer and in spite of an operation never really recovered. On Mondays John was given a lift to Glasgow by a member of the congregation who had business in the city every week. It meant a 6 am start and a long tedious drive. From there he caught the train to West Kilbride, spent a few hours with his parents and returned by the same means, often getting in well after eleven at night. It was an exhausting regime both mentally and physically for him, as the journey in the small white van was long and sick-making. Sometimes in the holidays he took Alison with him. After about a year his father died and he brought his mother to the rectory. She had to sleep in a bed in his study which was uncomfortable for her and inconvenient for John. Eventually they found a care home for her in West Kilbride but it was never really satisfactory.

Meanwhile Betty's mother also got seriously ill and she spent as much time as was possible in Fortrose looking after her for a few precious weeks until she had to go into hospital where sadly she died aged only 67. It was a miserable time for them all.

Without their parents' homes to go to, they had their first proper family holiday together in the summer of 1965, an exchange of sink and pulpit in Pately Bridge in Yorkshire. Jeremy and Alison piled into John's father's tiny Austin 7 while Michael and his friend Gavin bicycled the long journey and they took over the vicarage for three happy weeks. It was somewhat fraught for Betty because the vicar was on his honeymoon and the vicarage was stuffed with wedding presents. Alison discovered the bride's shoe closet and spent a lot of time trying on all her shoes. How could anyone, they all wondered, have so many pairs. This was to be the pattern of their holidays for the next seventeen years. John would begin the negotiations in January and they would end up sometimes in the 'gin and jaguar' belt in Sussex, sometimes in the industrial suburbs of Manchester. It actually didn't much matter where because there was always something to do and more importantly nothing that had to be done.

After seven years at Galashiels John received a letter from Canon Dobson, the Rector of Fortrose, to suggest that as he was retiring John might be interested in coming north to take over the Black Isle churches from him. John was. He knew the parish well, which included the whole of the Black Isle with a smaller church in Cromarty, because he had often taken services for Canon Dobson over the years. It seemed ideal from Betty's point of view because her mother was getting frailer, also she knew most of the congregation and loved the church where she had been married. The boys were now both at Glenalmond and Fortrose was an ideal holiday place for them, the rectory - the Deanery, as it was called - was big enough for them all including one of Bunty's sons in the holidays (she and Peter were still in Ceylon) and its situation by the sea stunningly beautiful. She could not believe their good fortune.

John was also delighted. The main reason, as far as he was concerned, was the churchmanship. Fortrose was considered in church parlance to be 'high'. The principal Sunday service was Sung Eucharist not Matins, which he had always wanted but never had either in Orkney or in Galashiels. The majority of Episcopal churches in the sixties were still thirled to mid-morning Matins so he was greatly looking forward to his new ministry.

Reflections

Everyone, in my opinion, is gifted with at least one vivid experience of God in a lifetime. Whether we recognise it as such is up to us. I had mine during those seven hard years at Gala. And they were hard years for both of us. Money was painfully short, the children at expensive ages and where the congregation in Orkney had regarded the Rectory family as not exactly a charity but grateful for hand-outs, the Gala folk saw us as not exactly wealthy but undoubtedly better off than they were and thus expected the hand-outs to come from us. The currency changed to decimal while we were in Gala and I solemnly swear to you twelve pennies in a shilling went a lot further than ten.

Orkney had showered us with rabbits, lobsters, whisky, geese, trout, an entire baby layette and even provided a home-help after Alison was born. In Gala there was nothing. I had no income of my own. I would have liked to get a job and made inquiries but my university qualification on is own was not enough for me to find employment as a social worker. It never occurred to me that I might get work in a supermarket like Joanna Trollope's *Rector's Wife*. There were no supermarkets at that time. Out of John's stipend I had £5 a week for housekeeping and it never stretched quite far enough. The boys had next to no pocket money. But - but the extraordinary thing was - there was always enough.

When dear old Mrs Baird next door died, Mr Baird came for lunch twice a week and paid us a pound, a considerable sum in those days. Once a cheque for £75 arrived out of the blue. A friend of my mother had had an unexpected windfall and divided the sum between the three clergy wives she knew. I remember sitting down on the bottom stair with the cheque in my hands weeping with gratitude. When it came to buying Michael's uniform for Glenalmond, my godfather took care of the considerable bill. Once when we were on the cusp of debt, my grandmother's engagement ring fetched a hundred pounds. When the time came to say goodbye to Gala, the cheque John received from the congregation more than covered all the outstanding bills. Yes indeed, looking back on it now, it is an amazing fact that there was always enough. And it was not as if we deserved it. Both of us were extravagant by nature, perhaps not having enough respect for money. John was possibly worse than I was, but, as it was usually me he spent his money on, I never protested, at least not hard enough. The fact that there was always enough was a small miracle in itself.

During our time at St Peters, John initiated a Week of Mission. A priest from Edinburgh (Father George Martineau) conducted it and as a result I found myself encouraged and eager to go on a personal retreat to Walkerburn.

My mother used regularly to go to retreats and she would say, 'It's odd how fond you get of people when you don't have to speak to them.' I was to experience this fact for myself. I cannot remember the names of any of the other people with whom I shared meals and services and homilies for a whole week, but I do remember a blur of kindly faces and smiling mouths. And I most certainly remember Father Dennis, our conductor, who was, I think, a Franciscan friar.

The carefully structured days each included a personal session with the conductor and three hours off in the afternoon to rest or walk as one pleased. I found myself telling Father Dennis things I would never have told a soul. For example: I had inherited from my father a dreadful propensity to weep on the slightest occasion. It might be while singing the National Anthem or listening to Beethoven's Seventh Symphony (my favourite at that time). Or it might be reading *La Belle Dame Sans Merci* or something holy. Holiness and goodness have always reduced me to tears. They still do. I could gauge a person's spirituality by the fact that my eyes would instantly fill up and spill over. I also wept during rows with John, and he hated it. Father Dennis more or less told me how fortunate I was. Most people, himself included, were unable to cry. 'Lucky them,' I said flippantly but he told me sternly I should look upon tears as a gift from God. The gift of tears. I was never able to go quite that far but it certainly helped me to think a little differently.

During those three hours off in the afternoons, some went to bed, some weeded in one of the enormous gardens, I chose to climb in the Border hills that sheltered the little town of Innerleithen and the Convent which I had already learned to love.

Border hills are entirely different from those in the Highlands with their heather, scree and boggy glens. These mounds were rounded, grassy, cropped by sheep and notched by gentle burns. One day, with God very much in my mind, I lay down on the rounded summit of one of them and suddenly I was flooded in sunlight, but it was more than sun. It was not just warm, it had a personality that was both gentle and yet immensely powerful and it filled me with an unspeakable joy. Did I tell Father Dennis? I don't remember but I think probably not. It was too private, too beautiful to share. He might have pointed out that it was an exceptionally sunny day, that after a heady week of services, silence and spiritual directing, I was conditioned for just such an experience and I did not want to be talked out of my own miracle. I could do that only too easily all by myself. But I know what I believe I experienced and with the passage of time the memory only gets stronger.

As does the other more substantial experience which was to occur during our last months in Gala. During the April my mother was taken ill while staying with a friend of hers in Kinross-shire. From all that this friend told me, I knew it was serious. Leaving Alison with John, I took Jeremy and we picked my mother up to drive her home. To die. She had acute failure of the liver, 'yellow liver atrophy' as the death certificate stated. It was a nightmare journey for she felt sick all the way. She tried sitting in the back of the car, the front, stopping for lengthy periods, travelling at a snail's pace but nothing relieved her. Back home her own doctor called that very evening. He more or less told me she had three months to live at most. I tried with poor little Jeremy's help to take care of her. The district nurse was wonderful but after a couple of weeks or so she was pleading to go into hospital. Edgar Dobson visited meticulously and anointed her but I don't think she ever gave up hope. She had seizures. After one of them while the nurses determinedly brought her back to life, I pleaded, 'Please let her go.' 'We can't do that,' I was told firmly, but of course I knew that. I only asked because she was in such pain. I don't think at any point in her illness she wanted to die because after one particularly bad turn she said to me, 'I nearly died last night,' as if such a thing was incredible. My sister Florence came up with her youngest son who was still a baby. We took to spending the nights turn about in the little amenity ward adjacent to the big ward. During one of my nights I was awakened by a commotion next door. I ran through to the main ward, and was firmly shooed away. About ten minutes later, one of the nurses came to fetch me. My mother had died (as I had guessed from the sudden silence in the ward.). There she lay without the tubes, and the drips and the machines, flat on her back with a sheet drawn up to her chin and my God she looked beautiful. Her skin was smooth, her eyes were closed and her mouth half smiled. But she was not there. It was no longer my mother. I am sure to this day she was up above somewhere looking lovingly down on me because that little voice in my head kept telling me, 'She's all right. She's really all right.' And I knew she was.

I got into the car and drove around the Black Isle for a while and let the tears flow. At about five o'clock I rang Florence and another day began. I was sad, of course I was sad, but not for my mother. I was sad for me and for the rest of the family, especially Bunty who was in Sri Lanka. Her funeral service was lovely with all her little grandchildren present and her interment with my father in Milnathort in the presence of her two older grandchildren brought across from their boarding schools a great comfort. The church is perhaps at its best at times like this, a strong, comforting arm around the shoulders, an affirmation of life.

A year before we left Gala, the SEC appointed its first Overseas Chaplain, Leslie Drage, a wonderful man who literally worked himself to death. When Leslie died, David Bruno was appointed in his place and we particularly looked forward to his annual visits. Travelling round the world for part of the year and around the Scottish parishes for the rest of the time, his aim was keep alive the link between Scotland and the Overseas Mission churches. Seldom a month went by without an overnight stay and lecture from one of the trainee priests he would send over from India or Africa. The post lasted for just over ten years and provided the link then needed between the outdated nanny-ing of the Overseas parishes while at the same time giving them the support many of them still needed to enable them stand on their own grown-up feet. Remembering that awkward tea party in Nanyuki, this, I felt, was my chance to make amends by offering heartfelt hospitality to those overseas visitors who must have been cold and lonely and homesick so much of the time. I think, but cannot be certain for it may be wishful thinking, that Desmond Tutu was one of those visitors. If it was not him, it was someone very like him. I can see him sitting in my living room, laughing and talking, as delightful a personality then as he is today.

Thus those years at Gala both in the church and outside it were busy and often fraught There were times when I hated the church, disliked a God who seemed to view all humanity, myself very much included, as 'miserable sinners', a God who seemed mostly to be full of 'wrath and indignation' in a world where everything enjoyable, as the saying goes, either made you fat or displeased Him. But then I would remember that shaft of sunlight on the Border hill, my mother who was so much better a mother than I deserved, my daughter's chubby little legs as she hummed her way down the drive to school, and the doubts vanished. Most of the time, though, I just took God for granted.

Chapter Eight

The Black Isle

Leaving a parish was always a wrench even though she felt that by going to Fortrose, they were going home. Sadly though, her mother had died the previous May. She had known about the appointment but had not lived to enjoy having her oldest daughter settled in the same town. She had also known about Betty's first short story success, which in a direct way was thanks to her for she had paid for the teaching course. This had been written as an exercise for the London School of Journalism and honed to the tutor's approval and was the tale of a small Shetland boy which had been accepted by the Scots Magazine in the April of 1965. The publishers, D. C. Thomson of Dundee, to whom she would always be grateful (and for whom she was still writing book reviews in 2013) paid on acceptance in those days rather than on publication like most magazines, which made them particularly popular with penurious writers like herself. The cheque on this occasion was for £20. By chance she had had a second acceptance, that of a Nativity play which adorned the front page of the Sunday School Chronicle. She felt she was at last becoming a published writer.

They moved in early November 1965 - not the best time of the year for a flit - to the great cold Deanery, situated opposite St Andrews church which was built on a flat grassy sward close to the edge of the cliff that overlooked the inner Moray Firth and Fortrose harbour.

What a welcome they received. Being already known in the parish helped and most of the clergy in the Diocese of Moray, Ross and Caithness came to the induction service led by the Gaelic-speaking Bishop MacInnes. The only fly in the ointment affected John. Shortly before they left Gala, Bishop MacInnes had written to him to say that he had had a delegation from the Fortrose congregation asking that the Sung Eucharist on Sunday mornings be replaced with Matins and that he, the Bishop, had reluctantly decreed that this should be so. No one would blame John if he were to decide against taking the charge.

Change his mind? That was unthinkable because, like her, he loved the Black Isle. He was willing to accept the Bishop's advice with a good grace, but he was deeply disappointed. On the plus side, St Regulus in Cromarty still had the Eucharist as its main Sunday service and Fortrose might well change its mind when the congregation realised that Matins and Merbecke would never fill the church - or its coffers. And he was right. After the honeymoon period when the Rector can do no wrong and the pews are full, the congregation settled down into its usual 25 – 30 regular attenders on an average Sunday, with about eighty on the Communicants Roll.

That was without counting the children. Over nearly nine years in Fortrose there were never less than 20 to 30 in the Sunday School/Youth Club from toddlers to teenagers who came remarkably regularly. She taught the older ones, Bunty the younger, and the toddlers were looked after by one of the already confirmed teenagers. They met in the Deanery rather than the church hall after attending church for the first twenty minutes or so. As with the Galashiels children, she invited the newly confirmed youngsters into a Youth Club, twelve of them with three boys and the rest girls. Two of the boys became regular servers but joined in the numerous youth activities which always included a Nativity Play - she wrote a new one every Christmas - and a party, various fund-raising efforts, inter-Youth Club quizzes at which they usually got into the finals, visits to the Diocesan Youth assemblies, discos and one-off events such as pony trekking at Fairburn.

In the late sixties and early seventies rules about riding were non-existent. Some of the riding schools provided hard hats but not all, some children had ridden before but not all, including Bunty, recently returned with her family from Sri Lanka, where Peter had lost his job as a tea planter when the island claimed independence. There must have been at least fifteen children on that ride all a little nervous and all excited. The ponies set off in a long string led by the girl who ran the stables up into the hills

113

belonging to the Fairbairn estate above the River Conon. The mists descended. The ponies somehow became separated, half of them well ahead with the organiser, the other half trailing behind with herself and Bunty. Ponies like to stick together, so the stragglers, without instruction, took it into their heads to catch up. This meant cantering. It was a scary moment for none of the children were familiar with the bouncing, shuggling movement. Watching Bunty bobbing up and down, Betty became weak with laughter and Bunty, watching her, was the same. Only one of the children - Verity - fell off. As she scrambled to her feet unhurt her first words were, 'Please don't tell Mummy.' As if Betty wanted to tell her mother. (But of course she did.)

Other memorable adventures included a trip to the 'Gates of Negapatan', a folly of a monument built on Fyrish Hill in Easter Ross by one of the Munro chiefs, who had served in India, to provide his cottagers and clansmen with an income during the potato famine in the early 19th century. Having got permission from the gamekeeper at Fyrish to climb through the dense woodland to reach the monument at the top, they set off after church one November Sunday afternoon. It took a lot longer than expected and by the time they reached the top it was growing dark. She had not thought to bring a torch so it was a case of running back to the cars as fast as possible to catch the light. Of course they made a noise. Whooping and shrieking with the sheer pleasure of running downhill between the darkening trees, they incurred the wrath of the gamekeeper who had been keeping a canny watch. In no uncertain terms he told them to be quiet. 'Do you want to kill all my roosting game birds?' he shouted. 'Scare them out of the trees and the wild cats will get them.'

The children were quiet. Then Alastair piped up, 'Better the cats than the guns.' Amen to that.

Other trips included a day of canoeing at the Redcastle Marina, skating at Aviemore, hill-climbing on Ben Wyvis, swimming in Glen Affric, picnics everywhere. These were the days before the Health and Safety rules kicked in. Looking back on some of these adventures she reckoned that their guardian angels worked overtime to look after them all.

Discos were all the rage at that time. When the Youth Club members were all about the age of fourteen, they got permission from the Vestry to hold their first proper disco in the Church Hall. Great was the excitement as they planned the food and decorated the hall and issued invitations. Then on the morning of the party, a delegation led by her nephew Alastair called in on her at the Rectory. 'Could we please have the party by ourselves?'

After some probing she discovered this meant without adults present. She would think about it. Discussion went on through lunch. Neither she nor John wanted to disappoint the youngsters, yes, they trusted them but ...suppose there was a fire, suppose someone took in alcohol, suppose someone got ill. Alastair's older brother, Allan, a student, was staying with them at the time. 'I'll go, if you like.' In the end it was left that Allan would attend and she would spend the evening at Meadowbank opposite the hall and look in from time to time. Not all the youngsters approved. Three of the girls were very sniffy. 'I'm not going, if you're not there,' said one. 'Nor me,' said another. Instead they played cards and every half hour or so she popped her head round the door. The hall had been transformed to a murky red glow. Pop music blared as the kids shuffled round the floor and there was one of them, Alastair, in fact, in a deep clinch with his girl friend, all of fourteen years old. (They are married now with four children.) She had to smile for she had known perfectly well this was the reason they wanted to hold the disco on their own. Naturally those without boyfriends disapproved.

One of the many projects designed to raise money not just for themselves but for good causes was the Lent Lunch. Glasgow had its own diocesan social worker, Lilias Graham, who was already a living legend in the Gorbals. Together with Nora Trundle (Bishop Haggart's sister), they had initiated a scheme whereby children from the Gorbals in Glasgow were offered a week's holiday as guests of parishioners throughout Scotland. St Andrews congregation was keen to participate. Money had to be raised for the children's fares and for the scheme to be properly organised so a Soup and Pudding lunch was arranged for the first Sunday in Lent. The Youth Club would do it themselves and invite the

115

congregation to come. Probably the mums made most of the food but the young people certainly served it and waited at table and cleared up afterwards. It was such a success that it became a yearly fixture and enough money was raised to invite nine children and also a mother and baby to spend a week in July, the hosting divided between the Sunday School parents and any others interested adults. Betty and John had two of the children at the Deanery. Great was the excitement as the various hosts and hostesses waited at Inverness station for the Glasgow train to arrive. First to get off were two Glasgow/Pakistani little girls called Samina and Safina. Catching a glimpse of John's clerical collar, one of them clapped her hand to her mouth. 'Gawd, Ah've forgot ma Mass book!'

She and John had James and Billy. James was a very young six year-old who had never been in a private car, train, ferry or had a bath before in his young life. He was to experience them all in one day. He was completely silent, shivering a little when she took him upstairs to bath him. To her horror she saw that his little back was a mass of scars. She asked no questions but later he told her someone had put a 'banger' down his jersey. That night he sat silently as she washed his little body but before the week was over it was a very different matter. He could not wait till bath time. 'Ah'm James,' he declared 'and Ah'm swimming the channel.' Back and forward he slid, propelling the water in spectacular waves over the side of the bath.

What broke the ice with James was the somewhat subdued Labrador they were minding for a few days while the owners were on holiday. James took to the dog, slept with it and played with it. They befriended each other. Billie was at the other end of the age scale, a small but very wise twelve-year old. Billie had no problem with homesickness for his mother and baby brother were guests of another member of the congregation. He had to translate all James' chatter for his Glaswegian was too broad even for John to understand and he had attended Glasgow university.

Every day of that happy week the congregation arranged outings for the children, garden games, beach picnics, a visit to an old-fashioned farm where they chased the hens and had rides on the

116

old Clydesdale. Those first years of the Holiday Scheme were successful, and, on the whole, incident free. Friendships were made that were to last a lifetime, class barriers broken, memories cemented. The children mostly came from loving homes for the scheme was originated not so much for the children but to give their long-suffering impoverished mums a break during the long summer holidays. Later when the state SWD got wind of it and put forward needy, often violent and unhappy children for holidays, the parish families could no longer cope. Then the rules changed. Originally would-be hosts needed only two references, which included one from their parish minister. Latterly host families had to fill in reams of forms, undergo visits and police checks to prove they were fit persons. The spontaneity was lost.

In those early days mistakes were made of course, and a small percentage of holidays were probably failures. Looking back on it after fifty years, she realised some of them could have proved disastrous. What a risk those impoverished Glasgow mums took, entrusting their children to complete strangers, but they had learned to trust the church and above all Lilias Graham and her volunteers and that trust had not been misplaced. When in time it became Betty's turn to help organise the Holiday Scheme from the Glasgow end, she learned to marvel at its outreach, the generosity of strangers and the beauty of hospitality. In Fortrose as in other parishes it was to become an annual summer event. Members of the congregation who were not actual hosts invited the little guests to social evenings with games or a day's entertainment in their own homes. This was to continue well beyond John's ministry in Fortrose, just under twenty years in fact, until the scheme itself changed beyond recognition. Some of the children kept in touch with their hosts for years even decades to follow and have remained life long friends. More of that anon.

The Deanery was a lovely old house which they filled comfortably when the family was all at home and with a very necessary spare room for there were always visitors. It was however also exceedingly cold and, as she was soon to realise, more than a bit scary. That there had been a ghost, nobody doubted, though it had supposedly been exorcised by the bishop with bell book and candle in 1927. 'She' - the ghost – had been sighted by many including the local grocer who told Betty with glee that he had seen her peering out of one of the upstairs windows. Another Edinburgh friend could point to the exact spot where she had once encountered the little old lady in the white mutch and the black bonnet. The story was that she had been housekeeper to the Misses Mackenzie, the two elderly daughters of Alexander Mackenzie of Mackenzie River fame who had lived in Avoch House before it had burned down and then moved to the Deanery which had been their 'town house'. (At one time all the important Mackenzies had town houses in Fortrose where they would spend the winter, including the Earls of Seaforth who had built Seaforth House in Academy Street after Cromwell's men had razed their Fortrose castle.)

This ageing housekeeper, so the story claimed, had watched her son drown in Fortrose bay and had thereafter haunted the windows of one of the main bedrooms to the left of the staircase leaving behind an atmosphere of extreme sadness and depression. She had known the story but also believed that the old woman had been sent to her rest by the exorcism so had no qualms about giving Alison the supposedly haunted room because it was closest to theirs. She even pretended that the story of the old woman had been connected to the spare room at the far end of the passage beside the bathroom. Alison was to have scary moments in that room not helped by the presence of Ming, her beloved Siamese cat, whose hackles rose from time to time for no particular reason. When Alison went to boarding school a student friend of Michael's stayed for a night in that room and swore that he was wakened by a presence that came and stood by his bed and stared down at him.

By that time, she was prepared to believe him for she too had experienced inexplicable phenomena. They had been in the house for about a week. At around four o clock on a mid-November afternoon she was sitting in the kitchen writing a letter. The house was more or less in order, Alison at Brownies, John visiting parishioners. She had baked a cake that was now cooling on a wire tray. She felt warm from the Aga, happy to be there, not

118

thinking of anything in particular when suddenly she heard the front door crash shut. Heavy footsteps crossed the hall, strode up the stairs, reached the top corridor and marched down towards the bathroom which was immediately above the scullery next to the kitchen. She had thought little of it believing it to be John back from his rounds but there was no rush of water in the pipes and the footsteps did not stop. They continued to tread, heavy and menacing, up and down that top corridor. Goodness! she thought, John's in a mood. What could have happened? She put down her pen, walked along the corridor through the dining room to the front hall and called up the stairs 'John?' No answer but the silence was now so intense that the hairs on her nape lifted. She turned to look at the heavy oak front door. It was still locked and the iron bolt firmly in place. No one, but no one could have come through that door.

Then she was scared. She took to her heels, ran out of the dining room, down the corridor to the kitchen and out of the back door (the only one they used in winter) and did not stop till she reached the Brownie hut where she cowered in the dark till Alison was ready. John did not come back for another hour.

Thinking about it afterwards, she realised that she could not have heard the front door crash so loudly, it was too far away, nor could she have heard footsteps on the carpeted staircase. Yes, she could have heard footsteps in the corridor above but not such a heavy dread that shook the whole house. What she had heard had been supernatural. From then on the stories increased. Robert, the young son of the previous rector, had been too scared to go to bed on his own. The town was well aware that the Deanery was haunted. Michael and June who were living locally came up to stay in the spare room so she and Ali need not be alone at night when John was away on retreat and also experienced the footsteps in the corridor. Michael, taking his courage in both hands, got out of bed to explore the noises but could find nothing and no one. Betty was sound asleep.

When the time came for her to write about Second Sight (*Ravens and Black Rain*. 1985) she discovered that there is a Gaelic term, *taradh,* which translates as 'noises heard at a time of

119

flitting.' As she was to discover, this was not a particularly unusual event. Although she had been scared, her curiosity was aroused. It was to be even more whetted by stories of Coinneach Odhar, the Brahan Seer, a local folk hero of the oral tradition, who had been allegedly burned in a spiked tar barrel beside Chanonry Lighthouse for his supernatural talents.

The Brahan Seer....Every writer needs a bit of luck He was to be hers. It happened this way. Her great friend from school days, Jean Smart, came for coffee one morning. Knowing about her writing ambitions, she produced a short cutting from the Scotsman which read. 'Children's Manuscripts Required' and a box number. To please Jean she applied. The reply told her that the manuscripts required were to be in comic strip form for D.C. Thomson of Dundee, (owner of the Scots Magazine) who produced a string of cartoon magazines for children including the Beano and the Dandy. Instructions on how to present these stories were enclosed and an invitation to produce a trial single instalment. Within the week two Dundee editors were having lunch with them at the Deanery, one of whom was Mr Stamper of the Judy and for the next eight years she produced two instalments a week for him at the rate of £5 per instalment. An extra tenner a week made a huge difference financially to a family of five struggling to exist on the minimum stipend.

A graphic story is divided into little boxes each of which had to carry a strong plot forwards. Her job was to invent the story, divide it into the required amount of frames, number and describe each little picture succinctly for the D.C.Thomson studio artists, and to write the bubbles or any short narrative needed. It was a lesson in plotting that she never forgot. Sometimes she would create the story, sometimes Mr Stamper would suggest an idea. She turned the Greek, Roman and Celtic myths into comic strip form, and also all the queens and princesses of Scottish history. She wrote fantasy, sci-fi and schoolgirl tales. There were rules of course. The story had always to be told from the point of view of a girl slightly older than the average reader, reckoned to be about twelve, and controversial subjects were to be left severely alone. For example, she planned to tell a story about Ugandan Indians resettling in Britain, a very topical issue of the day. She would set it in a Scottish village where an Indian and a Scottish girl would become best friends. This was a no-no from the outset. She could (and she did) have stories about African, Indian and European children but the races must not be mixed. 'The parents wouldn't like it,' Mr Stamper explained. So her little bit of propaganda for racial harmony never got near the typewriter.

It was Mr Stamper who suggested a story about the Brahan Seer. Even comic strips need research so off she went to the library and found *The Prophecies of the Brahan Seer* by Alexander Mackenzie and from then on she was hooked. Here was a character who possessed all the elements of myth and yet was believed in by Gaels as if he were factual history. The ensuing story ran to about twenty instalments all written from the point of view of a teenage girl who befriended and defended the great man all to no purpose for he was duly burned for witchcraft on Chanonry Point, a mile from the Deanery. There is a corollary to the tale. Years later when she became a speaker for the Aberdeen University Extra Mural Lectures, one of her most popular subjects was Second Sight and the Brahan Seer. She was, on this occasion, at Ness on the Isle of Lewis. As the stories all came from the Gaelic oral tradition in the first place, she asked the audience where and when they had first heard of Coinneach Odhar (Brown Kenneth), hoping perhaps that someone would say, 'my Granny told me', but no. There were three teenage girls sitting at the back. One of them shyly admitted, 'I read about him in the Judy comic.' The story had obviously been re-issued. Well, she thought with amazement, we may not have the oral tradition as it once was but we still have the Judy comic. Alas not even that these days.

At the same time as writing for Judy which took no more than a morning at her desk, she was also writing local history articles for a Highland magazine, a couple or so of short stories for the radio, also a short series of toddlers' tales for 'Listen with Mother' and had completed another novel, this time a thriller written from a carefully planned synopsis. Although she finished it, she got no enjoyment from it and that showed. It barely hit the slush pile of some half-dozen publishers before being sent back by return of

121

post. She quickly learned that she could not write fiction from a synopsis. All the creative stuff had already been done thus the writing became a grindingly boring job. She preferred to write from instinct, letting the creation flow from her brain down to her fingertips through her pen onto paper. Often she would sit down at her desk not knowing where her story was going, letting the ideas flow out of her, rejecting some of course, directing others, but the words never dried up.

About this time she entered a competition for Radio North, a short story to be adjudicated anonymously by her hero, Eric Linklater, who for most of the year lived in Nigg across the Cromarty Firth. Her story won. The prize was a small sum of money and the privilege of reading it on the radio. Needless to say the story was based on the Brahan Seer. It was called *The Stone* and told of how his divining stone fell into the hands of an impoverished old woman and thereby changed her life. Reading it aloud on air was a mistake because she mispronounced his name. Kenneth Odhar should have been Coinneach O-ar. In Gaelic the 'd' is silenced by the 'h' as a number of listeners were quick to inform her. From then on she was determined to learn Gaelic so that she would not make such a crass mistake again. She and Bunty started to go to Gaelic classes in Munlochy where she learned at least the rudiments of pronunciation. (Some fifteen years later when and she and John had retired back to the Black Isle she would sit her Gaelic Learners O-Level exam and pass with a credit.)

She was also to turn *The Stone* into a one-act play for women which was performed by the Chanonry WRI. One of her friends, Chris Haxton, took the part of the old woman and brought her to life. The play was acted three times over the years but never quite so well as that first time with Chris, a brilliant actor, taking the star role.

Two further outcomes of that radio competition were to contribute to her theory of luck. The first was to have had the story taken up and published by the local postmaster, John Protheroe, and sold locally as a booklet; the second was to be contacted by the journalist Kenneth Macrae, leader of the Inverness Writers Group which she was invited to join.

This was to be her first experience of writers groups. She had managed to reach the age of 40 without having heard that such organisations existed. That was undoubtedly her second piece of luck. Every fortnight she drove over to Inverness with two others, Josephine Leslie, the acclaimed author of *The Ghost and Mrs Muir* now living in retirement with her husband in Rosemarkie and Barbara Cunliffe from Poyntzfield, who had been a film star and was still a beautiful woman.

The group was excited. News that a weekend school for Scottish writers, instituted the previous year, was to be held again in Pitlochry towards the end of March the following year. A scholarship was available which would cover all hotel expenses. Competitions on every aspect of writing adjudicated by established writers were open to all attending. The London publisher Constable and Co Ltd was offering a silver trophy for the best novel entry and the chance to have the winning entry read sympathetically by their commissioning team, though they could not promise publication. The price of the weekend was unfortunately away beyond her means. However she would enter for the scholarship, a short story, and hope for the best.

When news came that she had won the scholarship there was nothing to stop her going. She prepared entries for most of the competitions and hesitated over the novel. Which of the five completed manuscripts should she send? 'That one,' insisted her daughter-in-law, June, who had faithfully read all of her work. *Lent Term* was a fairly explicit love story about an affair between a priest's wife and a rural dean in Northumberland. She had written it quickly at her desk in the Deanery drawing-room while Andy Williams crooned *You're too good to be true* on the record player over and over again. She had not as yet tried it out on any publisher. 'Are you sure?' she asked June. 'I'm sure,' June told her firmly so she packed it off under the pen-name of Jane Eyre along with five other entries and began another novel, this time – wait for it! - based on the legend of Coinneach Odhar. She had long since discovered that the only antidote to disappointment when one book failed was to be half way through another.

March arrived. Two carloads of her fellow writers from the Inverness group were also going. Held in 'Scotland's Hotel' in Pitlochry, the Weekend attracted about eighty writers from all over Scotland including a contingent from over the border. So successful was it that in following years the attendance had to be confined to Scots only, at least until larger premises could be arranged. As the scholarship winner she was given one of the best single rooms free. That night during dinner and after the inaugural address, friendships were formed that were to last for the rest of her life.

Saturday morning was given over to the results of the competitions. Sufficient to say the name Jane Eyre featured among the winners in every class she entered. Then the novelist Hugh Rae, a Constable writer himself who had set up the competition with the Constable publisher, Miles Huddleston (who was actually present), got to his feet.

Hugh was a brilliant speaker and the audience hung on every word. He described each manuscript in detail, was brief and a little contemptuous of her vicar's wife and the dean, heaped a great deal of praise on a witty novel written about a Jewish housewife. Then he announced in reverse order the winners. After a few more digs at himself for having anything to do with a minister's wife and a dean ('a dean for God's sake!') the Constable Trophy was awarded to Jane Eyre. It was probably the apex of her writing life.

But the hurdles were not yet over. In fact they had only just begun. Publication day was set for the following year. She had been to London, lunched with that demi-god, Miles Huddleston, had a hysterectomy, and then, a fortnight before publication day she came back on her bike from the shops to be met by John on the doorstep of the new rectory. Two young men had turned up. 'They're from the People's Friend,' he explained, 'to talk about your book.'

She wondered briefly, People's Friend? It was hardly Friend material. Hey Ho! Who cares? And it was in that spirit that they both entertained the two young men. There was a lot of laughter, and, looking back on it, she and John were both vastly indiscreet. Photos were taken of them both under the ancient apple tree in the front garden, really good photos too. Goodbyes were said. Then, and only then did she think to ask, 'You did say People's Friend?' 'No,' one of them replied. 'We're from the Sunday People.'

Shock, horror. The Sunday People was on a par with News of the World. Not read in the rectory.

That had been a Tuesday. She had to wait till Sunday with the Sword of Damocles dangling overhead. Closing Sunday School early and sending her class with Bunty over to the church, she got on her bike and sped up to the paper shop. Her worst fears were realised. There it was, a double centre spread, photo and all, with a bold headline, 'My naughty book, says vicar's wife.' Had she really said that? She could not remember but she rather thought not, because she had never considered it to be naughty, frank yes, but perhaps they meant the same thing.

The telephone began to ring and continued all afternoon. Most of the congregation, the ones that rang, were supportive. Bishop George, newly elected, had also to field phone calls. They were not so supportive. 'What are you going to do about this dreadful woman who happens to be one of your clergy wives?' was the gist. He went so far as to issue a statement, a lovely supportive statement, but he had not read the book and asked to do so. Apparently, she learned afterwards, that they were taking bets in the diocese as to who the unfaithful dean could have been. That was a secret she was unable to disclose because of course he was a figment of her imagination. Unfortunately the Bishop, as soon as he had read the book, was convinced it was him. Unfortunate too that he shared the same Christian name as her Dean, but, as she tried to explain, the book had been written before he had come to the diocese. He was never entirely convinced. When she had protested about the publicity to her publisher, all Miles had said was, 'It's done marvels for the sales,' which of course it had. *Lent Term* went into a second edition almost immediately.

But, in fact, *Lent Term* was not her first publication. As the result of a series of her articles for the tourist board on Black Isle history, the Fortrose postmaster, John Protheroe, commissioned her to write a short account of the Black Isle for sale in his Post Office. She had great fun researching the history, parish by parish and called it *The Black Isle: A Portrait of the Past.* Two local artists, Alan Cameron and Francesca MacIntyre, a schoolgirl at the time, illustrated it with black and white drawings and it was launched with a party in St Andrews Church Hall in 1973. Revised several times, it is still on sale in the local Post Office in 2013. Local history was always (and remains) one of Betty's greatest interests.

Early mornings, from five-thirty until nine, she was at her desk writing. She was already half way through her novel based on the Brahan Seer. The mornings were given over to housework, shopping, cooking and coffee mornings either in the Deanery or with her friends. One afternoon a week she hosted the Work Party, the churchwomen's organisation that had been started by Doris Dobson. She was a hard act to follow, for Doris in her quiet way had been good at everything from playing the organ in church to sewing, knitting, baking and organising fund-raising events, not just in the church but also in the town. She was not only efficient, she was enormously kind and probably the most popular woman in Fortrose. Somehow people always left Mrs Dobson's presence feeling good about themselves. One of her many quiet kindnesses was to make Michael a sporran out of an old leather handbag for his new kilt uniform at Glenalmond. She made it so well that he did not have to feel ashamed of it. She did not have an easy life for the Canon, her quick-witted, fiery, impatient, arthritic, little husband, was not always easy to live with and she also had her father and two children to care for.

The Work Party, fortunately, had members who were also good with their hands. They met on Tuesday afternoons in the big drawing room which never really got warm enough in spite of the extra heaters and the coal fire and prepared for a Summer Fete held outside usually in the Deanery garden and a Christmas Fayre always held in the small church hall. The Work Party members with a handful of men did most of the work in the parish, manning the stalls, filling the flower rota, and scrubbing the church. Twice a year before Christmas and on Tuesdays in Holy Week they arrived with scrubbing brushes, polish for the pews, Brasso, vacuum cleaners and dusters to clean every inch of the building. The hassocks were all taken outside and with the bits of carpet beaten till the dust flew out of them. Betty's particular job was to scrub a portion of the wooden floor and then provide the everlasting tea. Most of the women brought cakes or scones, so a good feast was had by all in spite of its being Holy Week. Most of them turned up again to decorate the church for Easter or Christmas. Every year the congregation would exclaim, she amongst them, 'I've never seen the church look lovelier.' Nearly forty years later the members of the congregation have different names (though there are still a handful of oldies) but they still say the same thing on the major festivals. 'How beautiful the church is! I've never seen it lovelier.'

One member of the congregation cannot go unnamed. Beattie Rogers. She was sacristan, cleaner, door-keeper, candle-lighter and there was never a service held without her presence. She sat at the back at morning service and right in the front pew at Evensong with her two cronies, Jeanie V and Netta from Avoch. She came to most of the weekday celebrations too. Come rain, come shine, John always had a daily congregation and he was the first to say thank you to Beattie. The vestry saw to it that she received a small remuneration though she would gladly have worked for nothing.

Work Party outings, like those in Galashiels, were eagerly planned and anticipated, some ambitious in scope. No buses were needed because enough members had cars that could take at least three passengers. One year was never to be forgotten, they planned a trip to Applecross over the *Bealach nam Bo*. John had recently exchanged their car for an automatic Rover. She never learned to trust its gear system. Driving up the *Bealach* with its series of hairpin bends was a truly terrifying prospect considering she had three old ladies in the car. If they stuck, who would be capable of getting out and pushing? Once there, all was well. It was a lovely day and she bathed in the chilly water to the delight of her carload who told her she was 'awfu' hardy'.

Other trips took them for example to Pitlochry, Baxter's Soup Factory in Fochabers, the Wool Mill in Brora, Pluscarden Abbey in Moray. She looked up and wondered at the massive re-building almost completed. Somewhere up there she had a brick with her name on it sponsored by her godmother.

Ecumenism was the name of the game during John's ministry in the Black Isle. In the wider church, the Livingstone Ecumenical Experiment where the Church of Scotland, the Congregational, Episcopal later to be joined by the Methodists decided to share ministry in the new town while Multi-lateral Conversations on Unity inspired other local congregations and led the way throughout Scotland. There were four churches in Fortrose, Church of Scotland, Free Church, a Roman Catholic Chapel and St Andrews. Ministers' Fraternals and joint services with the C of S were held regularly. When it was John's turn to provide a speaker for the Fraternal he announced that Bishop MacInnes had agreed to come. 'He is a Gaelic speaker,' he proudly told one of the more erudite Presbyterian ministers.' Hah, that will be the Argyll Gaelic,' he was told dismissively. He was a Lewis-man.

It was hard always to keep a straight face at some of the joint services. Neither John nor Mr Macrae from Fortrose were small men. Somehow they managed both to squeeze into the high pulpit provided one sat and the other stood. She daren't look up during the hymns. It was the same in the Cromarty East Church with Mr Ewing

During one summer, her nephew Kenneth on holiday from the Edinburgh Academy brought a French boy to stay in the Deanery. He was a Roman Catholic so Betty gave him careful directions as to how to find the chapel. When they all gathered for Sunday lunch she asked him, 'How did you get on?' He replied, 'The Catholic Church is Scotland is not much like the Catholic Church in France.' 'How so?' they all demanded. It turned out that he had been to the Free Church. No indeed!

John's ministry in Fortrose was dominated latterly by the Bishop's insistence that the vestry sell the Deanery. Yes, it was a lovely house and the idea to her and to many others was heartbreaking but it ate up money which the diocese, let alone the congregation, did not have. Also its coldness in the winter months did nothing for the fabric and the roof needed attention. Bishop

MacInnes in his usual forthright manner told John to 'Get rid, lad.' With the proceeds of the sale a new custom-built rectory would be built at the foot of the extensive Deanery garden.

There followed two anxious years for John and the vestry. Secretly she hoped that no one would want to buy the Deanery but it sold very quickly, bought by the sister and her husband of a member of the congregation, an Irish couple, who quickly made themselves part of the community and who had enough money to do the necessary repairs and alterations. Meanwhile they moved into a neat little rectory at the bottom of the garden with under-floor heating, not impossibly big grounds and enough bedrooms to house the whole family. Fortunately the price received for the Deanery and the cost of the new build evened out at £7,500. That was in 1970.

Writing about it now makes it sound as if it was easy. Far from it. The builders went bankrupt half-way through the project. If it had not been for a very strong and hardworking vestry, the transaction might have gone seriously wrong. The congregation 'removed' them physically, carrying their possessions cheerfully through the garden to the new home. Somebody dropped the grandfather clock. She spent the whole day in floods of tears. However they ended up with a comfortable warm little home and no lasting regrets. Out of a full heart she wrote to the vestry to thank them for what had been a hard and nerve-wracking undertaking.

Although the building of the new rectory had taken up a great deal of the congregation's time and energy, parish life flowed on. Saturdays were busy enough. It was her job to check the flower rota because though they had excellent arrangers on the list, sometimes someone forgot. When this happened one day in June she biked down the Ness and filled her basket with blazing whin - not easy in spite of gloves. She thought the church looked lovely but several people told her with shaking heads that whin indoors was unlucky. Another time it was Sweet Cecily and Blue Bells hastily plucked from the Fairy Glen. The Rosemarkie shore yielded primroses and pussy willows for Mothering Sunday picked and bunched by the children themselves and duly presented to their mums the following morning.

Sundays were especially busy. The early Communion service at 8 30 was followed by a hasty cup of tea and a scramble to get to Cromarty by 10. One winter's morning he had a contretemps with a deer. Fortunately neither was badly hurt. Then John started a Sunday School at Cromarty which Betty took in the Victoria Hall. This meant picking up several children who lived at Eathie. With four of the D children, and the three M girls this brought the numbers up to about twelve. Then a hasty scramble back for the 11.30 Matins at St Andrews and, of course, more Sunday School. Somehow she managed to put a casserole in the oven before going to Cromarty because there were always one or often two extra visitors for lunch, including Mr V from Cromarty, who had then to be taken back again in the afternoon. She, and Alison too before she went to boarding school in East Grinstead, went to Sunday tea at four o'clock with Bunty's Aunt Madge with her son Allan, a retired tea planter from Ceylon and his wife Margo. Card games such as Poker Patience, or, if Alison was there, Old Maid or Rummy, were part of the routine. Then there was Evensong at 6.30 which she sometimes went to, not as often as she had done in Galashiels for there was supper to prepare before slumping in front of telly till bedtime.

Mondays were John's day off (apart from funerals) and they both saw to it that it was truly a day off and out of the parish. They would go for drives and walks, lunches out (Chinese were the cheapest at an unbelievable 35p for a three-course businessman's lunch) and occasionally the cinema if she could persuade John to go, he was not much of a cinema fan. His ideal day out would be a visit to Macrae and Dicks garage where he would examine all the second-hand cars and chat up the salesmen who quickly realised that he was not there to buy. Garages first, radio shops or watchmakers came second. She preferred the bookshops and the cinema but usually they avoided Inverness in favour of the Culbin Sands or over Struie Hill where there were no shops. They both had to compromise a bit on Monday afternoons.

There were parties of course. The congregation was a very sociable unit. Where tea parties had been the popular entertainment post-war, now cocktails or drinks parties were in. Nearly every week pasteboard invitations would arrive for drinks from 6 pm - 8 pm. RSVP. How John hated those drinks parties. It was not until he retired that he felt able to refuse. Not drinking himself, he would be collared by retired army or colonial officers and his ears battered by alcohol-fuelled confidences which he neither sought nor wanted to hear. Betty hated these parties too but for different reasons. She never acquired the knack of 'moving on'. Other people seemed to flow effortlessly from person to person, not her. She would find herself stuck with some equally bored or stone-deaf guest and there she would stand - you never sat down - for the rest of the evening. The longer she left it, the harder it became to move. Sometimes she would be rescued by a hostess who would take her by the arm and say, 'I do so want you to meet so-and-so ...' and there she would be stuck for another half hour while her new acquaintance would try not to look over Betty's shoulder in search of someone more interesting.

She was also fairly heavily involved in the Chanonry SWRI which she met all her town friends. One year they decided to enter a Speech Making competition. Groups of three were formed consisting of chairperson, speaker and a third to give the vote of thanks. Practise sessions turned out to be hilarious but nothing quite matched up to the day of the competition. Dozens of groups from all over the Highlands had gathered in the Town Hall, Inverness. As chairperson of their group, it was Betty's job to introduce the speaker in no more than three minutes who then spoke for five minutes. The chair then opened the meeting for questions and took one only before calling for the vote of thanks from the third member of the team which was calculated to take no more than two minutes. They had a long wait. Then it was their turn. She duly introduced their speaker Mrs Jean Smart 'who comes to us today from the Black Isle, Ross-shire.' Unfortunately the judges heard it as 'the Black Isle, Russia'. Jean fielded the forthcoming question ('all the way from Russia!') tactfully and with humour, but they didn't win.

Any spare time Betty had during the rest of the week was given over to gardening. The Deanery garden was immense but fortunately so divided into orchard, shrubbery and large trees that it was not impossible to keep tidy. An elderly neighbour, 'Old Vic', as they called her, would come and sit beside her while she dug or weeded and entertain her with stories of her racy past. John's job was to cut all the church grass of which there was a huge amount. The mowing machine was never really adequate and he would spend hours trying to coax it to start. In spite of being a Town Councillor for the last three years of his ministry in Fortrose, he was never able to persuade the council to take over the chore considering the great grassy sward was open to the public. Dean Iain McHardy, his successor, who had also been Provost of Invergordon Town Council, finally managed to achieve this and it has been the council's responsibility ever since.

One spring while they were still in the Deanery, she broke her neck. It was a cold day mid-January and Jeremy due to go back to Glenalmond. John had been going to drive him to the Inverness station because she so hated saying goodbye. Unfortunately a member of the congregation had died and the funeral director had arranged to bring the coffin into the church that morning which included a small ceremony which John had to take so she had to take him. Because the large ferry was having its annual service and there was no guarantee there would be room on the small replacement, she opted to drive all the way round the firth by Beauly. Off they set quite early with Jeremy strapped in beside her. She was well aware that the roads were icy though they had been gritted and she stayed safely behind a bus as far as Tore. When the bus stopped to take on passengers, she passed it and entered Inverness-shire where the roads had not yet been treated. Her concentration lapsed and she must have been going too fast. Anyhow they came to a bend in the road and the car skidded, somersaulted and landed upside down in a ditch. During that hideous instance which seemed as long as a thousand moments between take-off and landing she was able to say 'I'm. sorry, Jem, I've killed us.' At least that's what she thought she said. The next moment they were both upside down in the ditch. From that angle she could see the bus skid to a halt and some of the passengers get off and slip and stumble across the icy road. She and Jeremy seemed okay. A kindly insurance rep who was on his way to Fortrose gave them a life home. Jeremy was fine though shocked and had hurt his knee. Later that night she was taken by ambulance into Raigmore Hospital. She had cracked one of the vertebra in her neck. After a week in traction she was allowed home in a plaster which made her look like a nun. Many and feeble were the jokes cracked thereafter.

The car however was a write-off. That dear little car, a metallic blue Renault, had been the first car they had owned, bought from the proceeds of her mother's will. Fortunately with the insurance they were able to buy a second-hand Mini replacement for the parish could not afford to buy them a car. This was always a bone of contention with the diocese. The Bishop did his best to provide transport, but funds were limited. Canon Dobson had used his own small battered car during his ministry, but before him, the Rector had been forced to take a taxi to get to Cromarty. One of the previous rectors (the Revd F. Carlyle-Burton) had used a motor-bike and been killed at the end of Deans Road. Fortunately the diocese paid for John's petrol and his carefully kept notebook showed just how often he visited and where. When he did not need the car, Betty used it to visit two elderly folk in care homes in Inverness and took in a fly trip to the cinema at the same time.

A couple of years after the removal to the new Rectory, John was ready to move on. He had a strong belief that ten years in a parish was long enough. He felt he had done all he could and that the congregation would benefit from new leadership. He persuaded his friend and colleague Canon Iain McHardy to apply. Iain, a charming elderly bachelor, was uncompromisingly catholic and would not put up with Matins as a main service.

Both boys got married during their time in Fortrose, Michael to a beautiful girl called June from Fochabers where they were married in the Gordon Chapel; Jeremy to a lively Mexican called Laura whom he had met in London when he was at Imperial College and they were married from St Andrews. It was a shoe-string affair but none the less enjoyable for that. With Michael and

Jeremy married and Alison at an Anglican convent school in East Grinstead (which Betty's great grandfather, the hymn writer Revd John Mason Neale had founded), he felt free to serve an inner city parish for his last decade of his ministry. He told Bishop George who was understanding and helpful and who promised to sound out his relevant brother bishops. It transpired that two parishes were immediately available, both willing to interview him. One of these was Salford Parish Church in Manchester, which he visited and was tempted to accept. He showed Betty a photograph of a vast barracks of a building with most of its windows broken. He would have dearly liked to go there but realised that at 57 this was probably a job for a younger man. Then he visited the joint Glasgow East End charge of St John's, Baillieston, and St Serf's, Shettleston, and that was that. He liked both these churches and the rectory at Baillieston which was a fairly new build, but above all he felt comfortable with the warm, welcoming people. Best of all for him there was a Sunday mid-morning Eucharist. No more Matins. No more droning through Merbecke and - a huge bonus - a diocesan car to cover the two parishes.

Strangely enough when they had been in Orkney two members of the Baillieston congregation on holiday had attended St Olaf's. Betty had taken them on a sight- seeing tour and she remembered they had talked non-stop about their wonderful congregation, the numerous activities and the crowded pews. It had sounded too good to be true. Both sisters were still there and ready to welcome them with open hearts.

Leaving the Black Isle was harder even than leaving Orkney. For both of them. A fellow councillor and a leading member of the congregation, Miss Hay, suggested John put his name down for a council house so that they could return to the Black Isle when he retired at the age of 65, so he did. At the time February 10 1982 seemed a far future event but it was only eight years, so there was that at least to look forward to.

That last Easter Sunday in 1974 she spent the whole of lunch at Bunty's in tears. They had all gone for a walk from Kilmuir church to Craigiehow Cave in the afternoon and the Black Isle was at its most beautiful. She could hardly bear to leave. However the day came. They tranquillised Ming the cat, and put him in the back of the car and set off to arrive in time for the furniture van. They were both sad, yes, but also excited, challenged and charged with energy.

Reflections

So where was God in all this bustle and busy-ness? Looking back on it I suppose he was there in spite of the hurried prayers, the teaming mind, the petty and not so petty everyday concerns…. I can do better than that. I *know* he was there.

At that time there was a lot of moaning and discussion about clergy wives who were - or were not - expected to become unpaid curates. I even wrote an article about it for the SEC church newspaper entitled *The Clergy Wife – Poor Thing*, for that indeed is how many saw them, me too, probably. I was always one who insisted that a clergy wife should 'be herself' whatever that meant. I was very much myself. I did what I did in the parish not because I was a clergy wife. I did it because I wanted to do it. I enjoyed it. Oh yes, there were dramas. I caused the resignation of a treasurer because I bought an apple tree for the new rectory garden without consulting her. It was a talking point for about a month, I suppose. I may have taken over the Sunday School and the Work Party and the Flower Rota but I never allowed myself to be elected on to the vestry nor did I interfere in spiritual matters on principal. John had enough critics already. He didn't need me too. As he used to say somewhat bitterly, 'You don't tell a dentist how to pull teeth, so why does everybody think they can tell a priest how to conduct a service?' It's true. They do. Those dreaded words haunted him; 'Why don't you…?' Or worse still, 'I think you ought to know…' and worst of all, 'everybody is saying….' (It usually turns out to be just that person) Those are the pinpricks, and believe me, the clergy wife feels them keenly on her husband's behalf so why would she add to them herself? Oh yes, there were arguments, there were moods and there were differences of opinion but these were usually about family matters, bills and personal affairs, never, as far as I can remember about the services or the behaviour of the congregation. John had a rule, 'Talk about things, not people.' If I did let off steam about someone, he wouldn't answer. Or if someone in the congregation tried to complain of someone else or something someone had done, his words were always, 'Never heed,' and then he would ask a question completely off the point. It could be very irritating but I suppose people got the message.

Of course that didn't stop me enjoying a good gossip, but in the various parishes John served my closest friends were usually not in the congregation. I don't think I realised until John retired and we became part of a congregation ourselves just how much gossip there is about the local clergy family. I have my own opinion about gossip which I know is contrary to the beliefs of others 'in the church'. I think that gossip is the cement that holds a community together. I'm not talking about malicious gossip which is rightly called slander. I mean genuine interest in the affairs of one's friends, kindly questions, comments, concerned interference. I find people infinitely, endlessly intriguing and I like to talk about them, what makes them tick. John had a theory that gossip was a particularly female thing. Not a bit of it. I remember Michael telling me that he sat behind a group of ministers returning from a meeting. They spent the whole journey gossiping unkindly about one of their colleagues. He was surprised, no, appalled would be nearer the mark.

About the services; I always loved them, particularly Evensong when John played the organ himself. His first love was music and he was a superb organist. The quiet service with the appropriate canticles gave me a huge love and respect for the psalms which has never left me. All through our married life John would often ask me to say Evensong or more often Compline with him which gave me a familiarity with the prayer book words that sound so tame and thin in their modern translations. I still prefer the musicality of the 1929 Scottish Prayer Book and the King James Bible and though, nowadays I happily read the Jerusalem Bible I cannot abide the SEC's shortened form of Morning and Evening

Prayer. The same applies to the Liturgies. I much prefer the language of the 1970 revision to the later ones.

This first new liturgy booklet came out while we were in Fortrose. That year and for the preceding decade, changes in the liturgy was probably the most discussed topic in the church. Congregations usually have to be coaxed carefully into any sort of change and the new forms of service drove some from their mother church for good. In spite of sermons of preparation, discussion evenings and experimental trials, there was still a substantial number who believed it wrong to tamper with the time-worn words. John was not one of them. He welcomed the 1966 and then the 1970 little Grey Booklets, as they were called, for their clarity and compactness. He was equally happy seven years later to experiment with the Orange Book - the first to use modern English - and then in 1982 the Blue Book, with its 'The Lord be with you,' and its somewhat banal response, 'And also with you'. He even liked the New English Bible. But he was good at compromise. The 8 am Sunday service retained the Prayer-book Scottish Liturgy and became a refuge for some who were made 'physically ill' (those were their very words) by the modern language.

On the other hand he did not like the Kiss of Peace, that pew-neighbour hugging in the middle of the Eucharist, a ritual which had lapsed for several hundred years until brought back again by the Church of South India. If compelled to include it, he would get it over and done with at the very beginning of the service. Not being a particularly tactile person myself, I too have never much liked it or felt it to be particularly relevant. I remember my cousin Betty telling me that when the 'Peace' started in Harpenden Parish Church, her delightful husband, Harry, noticing an apoplectic colonel in front of him, leaned forward and whispered 'I could do with a stiff drink,' at which the outraged old man relaxed, and shook his hand.

I didn't - don't - much care for extempore prayer of any sort either, perhaps because I know I would be so bad at it myself I like to think it's because, in my opinion, Cranmer's words cannot be bettered. The longer I use them the more I love them. At the same time I do and did entirely recognise the need for congregational participation. The more the laity can do the better. This was just beginning during John's ministry in Fortrose and he was all for it. Lessons were read not just by elderly vestrymen, but also occasionally by women and children too. The time is surely coming when like the Mormon church we will have no paid ministry at all apart from a few peripatetic bishops and all of us become the priests we were ordained at baptism to be. Would I like that? Come to think of it, probably not!

Meanwhile the SEC continued, as it always has done, to find new ways to express its service to God and in 1966 the Revd George Sessford (later to become Bishop of Moray, Ross and Caithness) launched yet another policy for the congregations. *To Serve Thee Better* issued 'a clear-cut statement of churchmanship and beliefs written in plain English.' The basic themes covered Worship, Mission, Service and Offering. Nothing new really but a simple Rule of Life, a timely counteraction to the theological uproar which had been created by John Robinson's *Honest to God.*

It occurred to me then as it has often occurred to me since that the Church, whatever the denomination, where rural or urban, fundamental, evangelical or liberal, in its continual agonising over how to pack the pews, fill the emptying coffers, and, above all preach Christ Crucified, the God of Everything, was on a perpetual uphill journey Perhaps because it sometimes misses the point. Perhaps because it attempts to say things that are not always relevant. Perhaps because there are no words.

Chapter Nine

Baillieston

The Rectory at Baillieston had also been custom built, a bungalow with a study by the front door, a well-windowed sitting room large enough to hold parish meetings, which indeed it regularly did, and a minute dining-room which Betty commandeered as a study for herself because the kitchen was big enough to eat in. There were four bedrooms but only one bathroom the walls of which were scrolled already with mould. Somebody in the congregation kindly gave them a load of beige-coloured tiles for the bathroom which hung about for a while as there was no money left for decorating so they decided to fix them on the walls themselves. She stood on a chair in the bath which John held firmly - it was dangerously wobbly - as he handed her up the tiles. The wee room looked quite good when it was finished as long as you kept your eyes off the top layer and the corners which were uneven. In spite of borrowing the right tools they found that breaking the tiles was an almost impossible task and it caused them a lot of hysterical laughter. Nor, alas, did the tiles entirely cope with the damp.

But mostly it was a pleasant sunny house set in massive grounds which included, across the dirt lane, St John's church surrounded by a graveyard, plenty of parking space and at the far end of the lane a large, shabby, well-used church hall and a garage. The grounds also contained an acre of walled-in field which was mostly a pot-holed wilderness because it covered an old coal mine and was subject to subsidence. One of the walls was shared with St Brigit's Catholic School and the children would toss over their sweetie wrappers and any other rubbish so that the field became a dumping ground. It was one of her regular chores to go round the perimeter wearing rubber gloves with a paper sack, or failing that, bribe some of the Sunday School children instead. The front garden was mainly lawn with a border against the house. She had high hopes of that border but it was infested with Mare's Tail, a primeval weed whose roots go down into the subsoil and were ineradicable. The smaller back garden adjacent to the car park flourished a little better with gooseberries and rhubarb, but heartbreaking to tend as any newly dug soil was heaven to the feral cats that haunted the field.

There were three large areas to mow every ten days or so in the summer, the rectory garden, the edges of the field and the graveyard. Sometimes a member of the congregation would offer to cut the graveyard but somehow the offer was seldom repeated, the result being that they divided the labour between themselves. John always mowed the edges of the field, she the front garden and whoever was free did the graveyard. Mowing between the graves was a tedious business and would take a whole afternoon. She used to know the names on the stones by heart.

The only member of the family to hate Baillieston was Alison's cat, Ming. The tranquilliser had worn off by the time they arrived at the rectory for the first time. He shot out of the car, darted away, and, before she could stop him, he had streaked across all six lanes of the Glasgow/Edinburgh motorway adjacent to the far side of the graveyard. She took her life in her own hands to go after him but eventually caught hold of his quivering little body. He never settled and would spend most of his life curled up on a cushion as close to the gas fire in the sitting room as he could safely lie. Proud, confident Ming became a shadow of himself, afraid of the traffic and the alien cats outside. He eventually died, we reckoned, of a broken heart.

Next door to the rectory and towering over the street was massive St Brigit's Roman Catholic Church and presbytery. There had always been a warm relationship between the two churches. An apocryphal story told of how on some unspecified date in the past, the Bishop had threatened to close St Johns for lack of support. The then Rector had told his Catholic brother who had replied in broad Irish, 'We can't have that now, no indeed,' and when, the following Sunday, the Bishop arrived to break the news to the congregation, he found the pews packed with worshippers and changed his mind.

The priests, three of them, were lovely men particularly Fr E, the curate, who wore denims with his dog collar. He invited John and Betty to his 'last supper' at the presbytery before he left for another parish and spent the whole evening in tears. (He was only going to Motherwell!) The women of Baillieston were also devastated. Fr E had very modern ideas. When the mums tried to confess that they practised birth control he would refuse to listen to them. 'Just don't tell me,' he would advise them. 'I don't need to know.' He was also delightfully naïve. He once said to Betty in all seriousness, 'You may have a small flock but they're all so loyal. How marvellous is that? We have more on the register than ever appear at Mass.' Duh? But had she not always thought that of his congregation?

A potential rift with his Roman Catholic brethren caused John some sleepless nights. The Easterhouse Orange Lodge members had asked if they might hold their annual church service and parade in St Johns. Always inclusive, John wanted to welcome them but the Orange Lodge, being a particularly Protestant movement, would not be welcomed in Baillieston by the Catholics next door. John rang the Bishop who advised him to put the matter to the Vestry vote. The result was tied, so, before giving his casting vote, John went to see the Canon next door. 'Welcome them in,' he advised. 'There are souls to be saved, and the best of luck to you.'

It was inspired advice. Several of the Orange Lodge members became good friends and regular worshippers at St Johns.

The Church Hall, though shabby and at one time rat-invested, earned its keep. Dr and Mrs Tinne looked after the Brownie Pack, a flourishing group of children who adored the warm-hearted, eccentric Tinnes who lived in a country cottage a few miles out of Baillieston. Every year they invited the congregation in groups to pick raspberries and there were always enough to go round. Dr Tinne was the chief consultant and specialist in tuberculosis, a disease still prevalent in Glasgow.

Alcoholics Anonymous took up another evening, the Youth Club, the Sunday School and most weeks there was either a coffee morning, a Beetle Drive, a disco or a Jumble Sale. The latter was particularly popular. Dealers in vans would come from all over Glasgow and expect to cream off the best of the stuff for a minimum price. It took an iron fist to hold them at bay for there were also a flock of regular customers who relied on the goods.

One mum in particular with five children was always among the first to arrive in the queue. During a visit to this family who had recently been decanted into a four-bedroom house in Easterhouse she was not so sure of their proclaimed neediness. She was just a little surprised when Mrs C showed her proudly round the new home to find one room unfurnished except for a couple of dog-baskets and two sleek and jacketed greyhounds. 'They're jist pets,' she explained hastily. Well, what else could they be, she wondered, but knew. While sharing a cup of tea in the living room, she was recounting the sad tale of her car radio stolen that morning in Bridgeton, when the unemployed dad, who usually hid behind a newspaper by the fire, suddenly came alive. He crossed the room and opened a drawer. It was full of car radios. 'Would this do you?' he asked, holding one of them up. She nodded dumbly. 'Right then,' he said. 'I'll get the lad to fix it for you. Gi'es us yer keys.' He cocked a thumb at his teenage son who picked up the radio, grinned at her and disappeared. When she left, a far posher car radio was blaring *Mr Bojangles* loud enough for the street to hear.

When John and Betty arrived at St Johns there were three women's organisations, a small but tenacious Mother Union who met in the Church vestry, a trendier group for younger couples and the CWMA (Church Women's Missionary Association) which raised money for the Chanda Mission in India and St John's Diocese in the Transkei, South Africa. In her wisdom or lack of it, Betty thought to unite all in a Work Party, run along the lines of Fortrose and held weekly in the Rectory. It didn't really work. In the end there were four groups, young women who helped with the Sunday school, Mother's Union, CWMA for which she was on the central committee that met quarterly in Edinburgh and the Work Party. Mostly the membership of all four overlapped, the congregation being small, which meant numerous outings, parties and fund-raising efforts. All eventually came together in a Christmas parish outing to the pantomime, a summer parish picnic which included the Sunday School and an Annual Summer Fayre, a huge event held in the field.

Some of those outings were memorable especially the ones with the younger women and Sunday school teachers. Brian, a young lad who had gone through Sunday school, Youth Club and was everyone's friend was working as a sous-chef at the upmarket Albany Hotel. This was a great place to eat as you could have as much meat as you wanted of every variety for a fixed price and Brian was in charge of carving the pork. Wine was flowing freely and every so often Brian's voice could be heard booming over the heads of the other somewhat surprised diners, 'Another wee swallie, Maureen?' or 'Evelyn' or 'Mrs M'. On another occasion they went to a hypnotist show in the Empire. Because there were about seven of them they squeezed into a box. The hypnotist decided to treat it as the royal box and continually bowed to Evelyn, who was sitting in the middle, to 'Beg pardon .Ma'am,' for some risky remark.

The final summer outing just before the school broke up was the Sunday School picnic with its races and prizes, usually held in the seaside town of Troon firstly on the beach and then for tea and games in the church grounds. The bus journeys resounded to the usual songs from 'Mr Marshall, show a leg..' until everyone's leg had been inspected to, 'Ye canny throw yer Granny off the bus,' all yelled at the tops of their voices. It didn't really matter if it rained or blew a gale. There was always the church hall as a last resort.

Then the time came for that much-needed summer holiday. John would start preparing in January by trawling through the adverts in the Church Times that read 'House for Duty' or 'Holiday Locum Required'.. He liked to take his annual three paid Sundays (more if the Rector himself covered the cost of a locum) together, but who with children, on a rector's stipend, could afford the Spanish Costa or even a cut-price camping holiday? When their parents had been alive, it had been their custom to go to Fortrose or West Kilbride for most of August but since 1965 this had not been possible. While in Fortrose, they had a fairly wide choice of destination from Edinburgh to the 'gin and Jaguar' belt in East

Suffolk. From Baillieston it was less easy. Not many priests fancied a holiday in Glasgow in spite of its proximity to the Clyde coast and the Campsie Hills so they spent several years in the suburbs of Manchester and Birmingham, once at Orrel near Wigan and a couple of years running near Selby in Yorkshire where they were joined by Michael and Jeremy and their own small families. But even city parishes had much to offer not the least being no demanding telephone

Once the children were old enough to do their own thing, a pattern emerged. She would get up early and write all morning, breaking the back of a new book in those three weeks. John would have a long lie, a leisurely morning and then they would spend the rest of the day together sightseeing, walking, reading and eating out

A few days after they arrived at Baillieston she received a phone call from a very old acquaintance of her mother's generation asking if she would be interested in becoming part-time assistant to the SEC Social Worker, Sister Beryl Straw CA who organised the SEC Adoption and Fostering Society. She would, she would! In which case she should ring Sister Straw who would fill her in and sound her out about what the job entailed and whether she would be a suitable candidate.

They met at a café in Glasgow. She liked Beryl, a Church Army Sister, immediately. Though very different in personality - Beryl was reserved, scrupulously efficient and tidy for a start - she must have thought Betty would do. She asked searching questions about legalised abortion. Betty gave her honest opinion. It was a subject very much in the news at that time, and had been discussed several times in St Andrews parish so she had worked out well in advance what she thought. 'I would try and persuade the girl to think very carefully about her decision, offer her every support if she decided to go through with the pregnancy. I would be there for her, enable her to have her baby safely and keep it if that was what she wanted, or place it for adoption if that was her choice. If, knowing all the options, she still decided to abort, I would stand by her decision and continue to support her through that painful time.' She had to make that clear because it was what she truly and

144

strongly believed, that the girl, knowing all the facts, had the right to choose for herself.

A week or so later she was summoned to Grosvenor Crescent in Edinburgh, headquarters of the SEC (in those days still the Representative Church Council, nowadays the General Synod) where she was interviewed by members of the Social Service Board soon to become the Board of Social Responsibility. Beryl told her later that no one on the Board had heard of her and the convener's (Canon A O Barkway) description had been terse to say the least. 'She writes,' was his only comment. *Lent Term* was still doing the rounds. Nevertheless she was offered the job of part-time Assistant Social Worker at half the minimum stipend and her own car. How unbelievable was that.

The first thing to make clear is this. There is no such thing as a part-time social worker. She had one day off in the week, John's day off, Monday, which they both tried to keep sacrosanct. Otherwise she juggled the hours to fit everything else in.

To begin with this included three mornings in Beryl's basement Edinburgh office. She drove through in her new Mini (the only stipulation in choosing a car was that it had to be big enough to hold a carrycot) and she and Beryl discussed the applications, wrote up case histories leaving the afternoons free for visiting the homes and getting to know the would-be adoptive parents as well as the pregnant girls. As the applications could come from all over Scotland they divided them out regionally. Beryl took the East Coast and the Highlands, Betty, Strathclyde and the Borders.

After a few months, the wastage of energy and time spent in driving through to Edinburgh convinced the committee that Betty would be better with her own office in Glasgow. Although Lilias Graham was no longer working in the Gorbals, she still had a huge influence on all the city social work done in the name of the SEC. She had opened her family home at Braendam in Stirlingshire as a refuge and retreat for Glasgow families with multiple problems and in need of respite. It was thanks to her and her volunteers, in particular Elizabeth Anderson, Convener of the Diocesan Social Service Board, married to Fr Boyd, John's former fellow curate at Old St Pauls, that Betty was offered a room in the sixteen-bedroom ex-rectory next door to the disused Christ Church in Bridgeton in Glasgow's East End. This enormous building at 192 Crown Point Road which had once been a centre of Episcopalian parish life accommodating four priests and six Lay Readers, had become redundant. Here from 1919-1936 the McBain brother priests had run a thriving Anglo-Catholic congregation, much of it drawn from the Episcopalian victims of the Highland Clearances, with crucifer, choir and bagpipes. The McBains had been followed by Canon Willie Cooper who had been one of Betty's father's favourite curates at Dundee. By the 'sixties, however, the huge local tenement population had mostly been re-housed in peripheral estates such as Easterhouse, and Christ Church sadly had to be closed. The rambling clergy house was now occupied by District Three of the Glasgow City Social Work Department.

The senior social worker, Mr Alec Calder, had a respect for voluntary societies believing their work to be largely preventative. Having no statutory powers to remove children or benefits, Betty and the other volunteers had access to troubled homes and were often able to deal with all sorts of problems before they reached crisis point. She, in turn, had a huge respect for Mr Calder and the other state social workers, who, she could see for herself, devoted their lives to their clients.

It was thanks to the State SWD that more babies became available for adoption. As Mr Calder said, 'We know of the children, you have suitable prospective parents'. She worked in tandem with one of the state workers over a couple of adoptions. It was true that the SEC always had a file of well-prepared parents but the supply of babies was scanty. The Roman Catholics and the Presbyterian churches both had their own adoption agencies, and so, of course had the state. St Francis Catholic Nursing Home, scrupulously correct, would pass on any Protestant pregnant girl who had gone to them for refuge. These were mainly Irish girls who had, to use the old euphemism, 'got themselves into trouble'. However, with the new legalised abortion law there were less and less babies available. The writing for private agencies was on the wall. Much to Betty's disappointment, the SEC decided to give up their Fostering and Adoption service and sadly Beryl left to take up a new post in Germany.

By that time, however, Betty had built up a large caseload of people who had nothing to do with adoption and fostering. These were either friends of Lilias Gaham or recommended by them, and their heart, run by Elisabeth, her daughter Jane, Molly Fisher and their friends, was the Good Neighbour's Club. This met on Tuesday afternoons in the old clergy house alongside Area Three and the meetings were attended by over fifty local women and their toddlers, many of them clients also of the state. It was precisely what it said it was, a gathering of neighbours for chat, advice and, best of all, the Boutique, a second-hand clothing store which they ran themselves. Many of their children went on holiday through the Children's Holiday Scheme. Most of Betty's work latterly had been in Bridgeton, Barrowfield and the peripheral housing estates such as Easterhouse and Castlemilk so when the adoption agency closed, she was kept on as part-time Diocesan Social Worker and organiser of the Holiday Scheme.

Those seven years as Glasgow Social Worker including the two years working with Beryl were an extraordinary period of growth for herself. She learned about courage, kindness, tragedy and poverty. So many touching moments... She had gone to visit a long-time Good Neighbour who had cancer, a string of small children and an absentee husband to find her thirteen-year old son at home alone. Nick limped to the door and showed her his right foot, swollen and bruised and obviously painful. He had kicked a stone instead of a football. His mother was at the cancer clinic. Betty left a note for her, helped Nick into her car and off they went to Casualty. The traffic through town was dreadful but they were talking earnestly about space exploration, she remembered. Then as they waited at traffic lights he said, 'We're having a conversation, aren't we?' I nodded. 'I do like a proper conversation, don't you?'

Not long after this Nick's mum found in his room a radio which was not his own. A neighbour in the block of flats complained of just such a radio having been stolen. He owned up to being the thief. Apparently he dressed himself in black, fantasised about being the Avenger, climbed out of his window at night and broke into homes, mainly those of pensioners. He confessed to having stolen several radios.

Nick's family also had a statutory social worker. Together she and Betty plotted how to keep Nick out of the courts because they both believed his mother, being ill, could not cope with any more disasters. Betty got Nick to write a letter, a painstaking apology, while his other social worker visited the pensioner with the radio and letter and somehow managed to get her to drop the charge. Sadly it was not to be Nick's last offence. Two years later he was banged up in a young offenders establishment at Falkirk. Betty took his mother and the youngest half-sibling to visit him. What an eye-opener that was. She had visited before as a social worker and had been treated politely. On this occasion however, she was just another visitor. She and Nick's mum were scrutinised, searched, spoken to roughly, kept waiting and made to feel guilty. Betty was ashamed for the officers who would treat anybody, least of all the anxious relatives of young prisoners, so disrespectfully. Nick's mum took it all for granted. But Nick in a navy blue uniform, looked well. The acne spots had cleared, his eyes were bright and he was enjoying the sport. Incidentally Nick became a chef and as far as she knew stayed out of trouble for the foreseeable future.

There were tragedies too of course. The girl who changed her mind a week before she was due to sign the adoption papers and Betty had to take away the baby she had placed a few weeks before. The mum whose eleven-year old lad died of glue-sniffing. One heroin-addicted young lad told her bitterly, 'There's nothing in this dump to look forward to that's better than that kick.' And no. Looking at it from his point of view there probably wasn't.

Guilty moments: the woman who phoned her from a call box shaking with anger asking her to visit. She had heard on the radio that Jesus had not necessarily been born on the 25th December. 'They were lying, weren't they?' Betty tried to explain honestly and ended feebly, 'Does it matter which day it was?' 'Of course it matters,' she stormed. 'Is it all lies then? Good Friday and Easter? That's me done with God.' Betty left feeling miserably inadequate. It felt like she had that Biblical millstone dangling round her neck.

Humble moments: she had gone to visit Mrs S who had a husband with TB, two sons in prison and had asked for a holiday for her youngest aged nine. She herself had cancer. Betty found her lying on her settee reading a book. Reading and books apart from the *Record* and the *Evening Times*, did not feature much in the lives of the Good Neighbours. Betty asked her what she was reading. It was a Mills and Boon romance. 'It takes me right out of myself,' Mrs S explained. 'I do like a good read.' Never again would Betty despise Mills and Boon. She would have liked to think that one of her books would give someone a few hours of happiness. Indeed she tried hard to write a romance herself with no success whatsoever.

The Holiday Scheme took a lot of organising so she asked Joyce to help her in the office. Joyce and Jack were members of St Johns congregation and nothing was too much trouble for either of them. The organising started at the beginning of the year. Former host families had to be contacted, new hosts found through advertising and speaking engagements, references to be taken up. The hosts would say how many children, what ages and what sex they would like and what week in the summer would suit them best. The Good Neighbours applied for their children, and, through them, the children of their friends and there were always a few referred from Area 3 SWD. The children had then to be matched to hosts as far as possible, dates arranged and escorts found, usually from among the Good Neighbours themselves for the children could not travel alone. Tickets had to be booked and paid for. Then there was fund-raising, not difficult for people were incredibly generous, but it all had to be done. Without Joyce and Molly and Josephine and Elizabeth and many others she could never have managed.

So what was the point of the Holiday Scheme? Originally Lilias had started it in 1966 by writing to all the Episcopal churches in desirable locations to ask for host families. The initial reason was to give the harassed mums in the Gorbals a rest during the long summer holidays. The focus now had shifted. The aim was to give children who were not having any other family holiday a week's break from the city. Once on a visit to Easterhouse during the

Glasgow Fair Fortnight, she saw the point with a new clarity. Their mother was out and she was welcomed by two lads in their twenties, one of whom was unemployed and the other on holiday. She was welcomed as only Glasgow folk know how, a cup of tea was made and she sat between these two young men as they reminisced. They had gone on holiday together several years running and they sat there like two old men recalling their childhood. Those holidays were remembered, every moment of them. 'Do ye mind….?' said one setting the other off and then the laughter would come. .'Aye, we were no angels.' 'They were the best days of my life,' said one soberly and the other nodded.

So this is what it's all about, she thought. Memory building.

But it was more than that. Once little boy went to Leuchars to an RAF family. He was a very young seven-year old. His hostess told me afterwards that he had been terrified when her husband appeared in uniform. The little lad was an Irish Catholic and those were the bad days of IRA and terrorists and he was sure he had been sent away to be killed. By the end of the holiday he was confident and happy and boasting - how those wee kids liked to boast - about what they did and what they got.

So this is what it's all about, she thought; bridge building. 'Them' and 'us' had for one short unforgettable week become 'we'.

Of course not every little visitor settled. The organisers soon learned that those who had come from broken and violent homes were the most homesick, afraid that when they got back mum or dad would have gone for good.

There were other small disasters too. Most of the children loved to sit in their hosts' cars. On a hot day they could be seen, boys and girls alike, sitting in stifling Rovers or Renaults, windows tightly shut, playing their little games of fantasy. Most hosts were careful to remove the keys. One forgot. The car was in gear and leaped forward to smash the garage doors. No one was hurt. The Scheme was insured against just such accidents, so on that occasion all was well. A far sadder occurrence involved the return of a child. The family, a doctor and his wife and small son had been selected to host a diabetic child who needed injections, a dear little boy of eight years old. As was required of all the children, he had a doctor's certificate to say he was fit to travel and he had his instructions for the host doctor. Mostly these doctors' inspections were to check for head lice. With all the fuss over Davy's diabetes, the head was forgotten. He had lice. Most host parents were prepared to deal with this but not Davy's. The hostess went mad. She banished her husband and her own son to grandparents, fumigated the house and demanded Davy be fetched immediately. Poor wee Davy. Betty went for him herself. Fortunately another holiday was found for him almost immediately.

Homesickness usually lasted for twenty-four hours. A skilful hostess knew just how to distract her little guest. Phone calls home were not forbidden but carefully rationed. Betty and the other organisers were always at the end of the line to advise the host family, encourage and rescue, but it was rarely necessary.

Sometimes the host families complained that their particular little guest seemed not to need a holiday at all. A few, a very few, arrived with full purses, and, on one occasion, seven changes of knickers. It had to be explained to them that the full purses were the result of little gifts of a shilling or two from all the neighbours and some mums beggared themselves to send their children away tidy. Mostly they left home with a plastic bag containing a torn pair of shorts or a pair of battered tennis shoes. Then all came home a week later rosy-cheeked and smiling with new bags bulging with goodies from cakes and jam for Mum to complete new wardrobes, bubbling over with their experiences and eager to be put on the list for next year. Whenever Betty saw them in Dalserf Street or Crown Point Road or indeed anywhere she happened to be visiting, children would cluster round her car, demanding to know could they get a holiday.

Having broken into the world of publication several years before their move to Glasgow, Betty was not willing to give up her writing life which constituted along with the parish and her social work, at least a quarter of her time and energies. Being a morning person, Betty soon realised that if she were to continue to publish, it would mean an early start. So for the next eight years she rose at 5.30, had three hours of peace at her desk with a second-hand

Remington typewriter, wrote till 8.30, and then for the rest of the day forgot about her writing. It still left the occasional evening free for Corrie. Writing novels was a lengthy business for she found she could not create straight on to a typewriter, so the first draft was by pen, hastily transferred on to the typewriter because her handwriting was illegible, followed by at least three further drafts before she was satisfied. She allowed herself three errors on every page carefully typex-ed correct. The most frustrating thing was putting the carbon paper in the typewriter the wrong way round. It happened far too often because she was always in a hurry. She was such an inaccurate typist that when she had begun to earn a little more, she would send the final draft to a professional typist at a cost of £100 for two copies. It was worth every penny.

In those eight years at Baillieston, she published four more novels, one of which *The Seer of Kintail* reached the best-seller list in the Scotsman, the next, *Hannah Hereafter* won an Arts Council Book Award. The third, *The Eye of God* told the story of the historical Brahan Seer and was ruined for her and for her sales by the crudeness of the cover. Her protests were largely ignored. This was followed by what she hoped would be the most important of her historical novels. It described the fortunes of a young Highlander who having been evicted from a Highland glen during the Clearances, travelled to America where he in his turn evicted a family of native Americans. Her publishers were not enthusiastic and she had to cut the novel to half its length, thus, in her opinion, killing the story stone dead.

Her agent in those days, Murray Pollinger, found her. Shortly after *The Seer of Kintail* was published, she had letters from four agencies all offering to handle her books. After consultation with her publisher, Miles Huddleston, she chose the Pollingers because they were his trustworthy friends. Murray was a bit scary, tall, dark and thin, clad in a long black overcoat. On one occasion he ticked her off like a schoolgirl for delivering by hand a manuscript which had been printed in dot matrix with the pages still linked to each other. She was made to sit down in his office and separate them out and then he took her out to lunch striding ahead of her across the street his black coat flapping at his heels.

For each publication there was a launch, a signing session, TV appearances and she was duly wined and dined either in London or Glasgow. Her first publisher's lunch in London was a nerve-wracking affair. Her publisher, Miles Huddleston, was the kindest and handsomest of men but seemed as shy as she was. He fortified both of them with a double gin before they ate which was not a good idea. Betty could hardly walk into the restaurant. When confronted with the French menu, she was stumped. 'You choose,' she said. It was the first time she had tasted avocado which because it was doused in vinegar, she hated and could hardly swallow. She did a lot of giggling, that much she remembered, and also that they had the most delicious goujons of sole.   Meanwhile John and Alison (for this was during the summer holidays) ate happily at a Spaghetti House.

Constable employed several reps who went round the country flogging their lists to the various outlets. The rep for the north of England and Glasgow was called Derek. He was one of the nicest of men and she and John always enjoyed his visits. He would bring with him proof copies of new detective thrillers from the Constable list which John enjoyed and relate all the latest gossip about her fellow Constable authors. It was his job to persuade bookshop managers to buy *The Seer of Kintail*, his idea, gleaned from these sessions that there should be a new edition of Alexander Mackenzie's *Prophecies of the Brahan Seer*, his suggestion that she should be commissioned to write it and his 'word with Miles' that clinched the deal. The book was a collection of tales from the oral tradition gathered by Mackenzie in 1897 about Second Sight and the Highland Seer, Coinneach Odhar. The few remaining original copies had a waiting list in the Highland libraries for never less than sixty readers. She was happy to accept the commission for an outright sum and a small but fair share in the royalties. All she did was to bring each of the original prophecies and their possible fulfilment up to date without changing the original text in any way, and add her own introduction and afterword It had been an inspired suggestion for the book has gone into many editions and is still in print thirty-five years later.

It was, however, her third book, *Hannah Hereafter*, that was to seal her future as a writer. The theme was complicated, to do with honesty and self-awareness and she struggled. Without the advice and mentorship of Hugh Rae it might never have succeeded in gaining a Scottish Arts Council Book Award. What had pleased her most was the reaction of her reader at Constable, the undoubtedly formidable Peter Day, who had been given her book to look at. He had been so impressed that he had written to her personally and sent the letter off with a £5 stamp so that it would arrive the next day. Peter was to become a valued friend.

So her life as a writer was important to her. It was also put into perspective by the mother of one of her adoptive parents, a black naval couple from the States stationed at Faslane. On one of her routine visits, which happened to be the day after her appearance on the Scottish TV News talking about the publication of *The Prophecies of the Brahan Seer*, the adoptive father's parents from Alabama were on a visit. Tall, reserved and polite, the new grandmother had turned to her. 'So you write, honey?' she had said graciously. 'What a pleasant little pastime for you.' Yes indeed.

Family life too had a very special share of her time. Jeremy, Laura and Baby Shakti had moved down to Gourock where Jeremy had got a job mending tellies for the Co- op before finding employment with the American company, National Semi-Conductors who had opened a factory in Greenock. Here he was to find his niche professionally, move at their expense to their headquarters in Silicon Valley, California, and rise to be one of their top engineers. In the seventies, however, though they were as poor as church mice, both of them managed to make the most of their stay in a council estate and it was there that their second little girl, Mayva, was born. Most weekends they managed a visit to Baillieston and one of Betty's delights was to play imaginative games with her grandchildren in the churchyard. Barbara Woodhouse and her dogs who featured frequently on telly, fascinated the little girls, so Betty had to be the bossy Barbara, while the girls turned into puppies who 'sat' and 'fetched' and 'barked' at her word of command.

Alison left her convent school in East Grinstead to become a boarder in an Edinburgh school where she excelled at music. She managed to obtain a course in Stage Managing at RADA and found herself a job as a stage dresser for a while at Edinburgh. Michael who was teaching in Aberdeen and his little family of Graeme and Ania came through when funds allowed and they often spent their summer holidays sharing the same vicarage holiday accommodation.

Sundays were as busy as they had been in Fortrose for John had two churches to serve, St Johns and St Serfs in Shettleston while she had Sunday School and older members to fetch from Coatbridge or Uddingston by car. Usually they had guests for lunch. It was a matter of putting the meat and potatoes in the oven before church and hoping for the best. Casseroles could be happily ignored and usually turned out fine but roasts were trickier, often vastly overdone but as John preferred his meat to be tough and overdone rather than tender and rare, there were no complaints.

Two occasional Sunday guests were the A's from India. Mr and Mrs A had a daughter who worshipped in St Serf's. While a nurse in one of the Glasgow hospitals she contracted an illness which left her close to dying. Her parents were enabled to find the funding necessary to travel to Glasgow to visit her and for a while were regular worshippers at St Serf. Strong Anglophiles and Anglicans they had ditched their Indian name for a British one and loudly regretted the passing of the Raj. Their English was impeccable and their manners a marvel. They did not, however understand British cooking and wanted to learn. 'Please let me prepare you an Indian meal and bring it to your house,' Mrs A offered, 'and I,' said Betty, 'will prepare you a traditional roast beef Sunday lunch for you.'

Mrs A looked beautiful in her sari and Mr A smart as paint in a lounge suit and tie. The two meals were to be served together. Both women exchanged plates. She received a very hot curry and rice and Mrs A a plate of roast beef, roast potatoes, garden peas, horseradish sauce and gravy. It was an extraordinary sight to watch these two delightful people eating with their fingers. More extraordinary was just how neatly and un-messily they coped with the slices of meat and gravy. They were vociferously polite after they had finished but did not ask for seconds. The curry was out of this world. John had a third helping.

So the years passed quickly until it was time to think of John's retirement from the active ministry. Although their name was down for a council house in the Black Isle, they now spent Mondays scouring the most likely places for a little house of their own. Thanks to shrewd stockbrokers, she still had most of the £10,000 left to her by her mother in spite of the fact that she had regularly to sell out to cover the cost of Alison's education at a boarding school in East Grinstead and latterly in Edinburgh. If they could find a suitable house, the church might be willing to invest in a new retirement property provided it became church property after their deaths. They looked in Dumblane, Kinross, Helensburgh, St Andrews and down the Clyde coast but when it came to making a decision, she knew she did not want to part with what little capital she had. They would need a car, not to mention a small nest egg to set aside for family emergencies.

About a month before John's 65th birthday he heard from the Ross and Cromarty housing department that a two-bedroomed, semi-detached house in Rosemarkie was available in Mackenzie Terrace. She drove up to see it, realised that they would have to get rid of most of their possessions including the two ancient Indian carpets that had belonged to her grandmother for the house was tiny in comparison with Baillieston, but it would do. They would have a bed-study each so that she could continue to write and John to say his office, study and listen to his music. They would share the living room and the kitchen. They would be back with Bunty and all their old friends at St Andrews church. John had already contacted Bishop George Sessford and offered to help out in the diocese. They would have to buy a car and a cooker... Yes it would do very well indeed.

Michael and Jeremy and Michael's brother-in-law John hired a van and after some heartfelt farewells, a party with presentations and a lot of tears on her behalf, they left Baillieston and parish life was over.

Afterword

If you count his curacy and the army years, John served seven parishes, each of them as different in quality and tone as they were in geography and tradition. Ripon cathedral was ancient and majestic, Old St Pauls was 'high' and glittery, the army chapels were 'low' and functional, the two Orkney churches were keen and lively, Galashiels was large and sunny, the two and a half Black Isle Churches, 'middle of the road' and beautiful, the Glasgow East End churches were enthusiastic and cosy. So what makes a parish? Not the church building, every one of which caused trouble of one sort or another. Dry rot followed us around like a bad smell. Dampness, coldness, leaking roofs and cashless-ness were perennial problems all of which had to be dealt with, and not just in the church. The rectories ranged from a cockroach infestation in Ripon to the extreme cold of the beautiful Black Isle Deanery or too small for a growing family as in Galashiels. At the end of a lifetime of ministry, rectory families are faced with homelessness. A tied house is not much use when the rector retires and has to find accommodation for himself and his wife with no capital saved from the pared-down minimum stipend and too small a pension to pay a mortgage.

Year after year someone would get to his or her feet (usually hers) at the end of the annual Representative Church Council meetings (now the General Synod) and plead that priests be enabled to buy their own houses at the beginning of their ministry so that by the time they retired they had the wherewithal to live in a place of their own choosing. Year after year those pleas fell on deaf ears. I know there are a few church-owned houses for retired clergy, other priests have inherited family homes or enough wealth to buy a little bungalow by the sea but most can't. We were lucky enough to get a council house in the county of our choice because John had had the forethought to put his name down for one in the Black Isle ten years previously. For a past rector to return to his old parish is not always thought to be a good idea for obvious reasons, but we had little choice. The Rector of the Black Isle when John eventually returned had two previous rectors living on his doorstep. It can't have made his job any easier.

Though it may seem like it, I'm not really complaining. Why should I? We always had a roof over our heads. However, I firmly believe that social housing is more suitable from the start for a priest and his family than pretentious and expensive old rectories, or smart, new, custom-built bungalows. It may well happen as congregations grow smaller and rectories sold as money gets tighter.

No, I am certainly not complaining because a parish is a great deal more than stone walls and a glittery altar. A parish is a small green oasis in a large windy desert. It is a quiet parking lot in a perpetual city rush-hour. It is a family which like all families has its squabbles and tantrums and sulks. Conversely it is an abode full of warmth and stability there to care for people in a special way 'through the all the changing scenes of life' from birth and baptism to death and burial. Until John retired, and not counting the university years, I had never known any way of existence other than parish life either at its centre or tucked within its folds. And yes, there have been times when I've wished our weekends could have been like everybody else's, when instead of gearing up for Sunday we could have wound down, but most of the time I was just too busy. There was always Monday to look forward to.

I have often wondered what it must be like to arrive in a strange town without knowing anyone, how lonely, how difficult to make a new circle of friends. For us, with every move, we had a whole congregation waiting to welcome us into their homes and into their hearts starting off with a big party and a fistful of invitations. We certainly tried to welcome strangers and incomers who had the courage to attend a new (for them) church, and it does take courage to risk sitting in someone else's pew, confront new faces and remember new names.

The analogy of the parish as a family can be carried further, for its children quickly became an extension of our own three, its oldies the grandparents we had never known, the vestrymen, sidesmen and servers our fathers and brothers, the single women, wives or widows our sisters and mothers. The grumblers - and do they not exist in every family? - John made wardens or co-opted on to the vestry. To stretch the analogy even further, we were soon made aware of how much parish families hate change. More than in any other organisation, congregations dislike changes. The departure of a familiar priest and his family, the removal of a piece of furniture, the omission of a dated word in a well-know prayer, the introduction of a new ritual, a different tune to a popular hymn, the modernisation of an ancient liturgy, these have all in their time caused members of the family to fulminate, sometimes withdraw and their loss always keenly felt.

This dislike of change is only too easy to understand. So fragile is the thing we call faith that the removal of a pulpit, the ordination of a woman or the inclusion of a gay ministry has sometimes caused it to tremble, occasionally to shatter. You try to explain that with modern audio systems, the softest spoken preacher can easily be heard from the chancel steps; that the Holy Spirit surely has the right to call whomsoever it wants to serve its ministry and that Jesus was not so picky, fear of change is part of human nature. Everything else in life is so constantly changing - work conditions, personal appearance, children, the climate, the economy - that we look for stability and changelessness in our parish church. My father used to say that as a priest you have a choice. Make changes right at the beginning of your ministry when the congregation is prepared to forgive you, or wait until you are loved then make them, but the truth is that as far as a parish is concerned there is no perfect time to make changes. The congregation has to be dragged kicking and screaming into today's world but it usually gets there in the (occasionally bitter) end.

Of the seven churches John served, did we have a favourite? If John had, he would never speak of it even to me, but I know he had a soft spot for Cromarty. As for me, I liked the different churches for different reasons. Orkney for its many young families like ourselves, because it had been my father's beloved home and for the intense beauty of the islands. Ripon Cathedral for the kindness and friendship of the Dean and Mrs Hughes, for the camaraderie of other clerical families and for the majesty of cathedral worship; the army for giving us Africa and Church

Crookham. Galashiels particularly for the young people and the Black Isle for being home. Glasgow too was special to me for the warmth of the congregation, and for the privilege of practising the career for which I had been trained. Seriously speaking, just as we loved our children equally, it was the same with the congregations which is not to say that from time to time we did not get cross with some of them, argue with others or get fed up with the whole lot, but we always loved them both at the time and in retrospect

However many mistakes we both made, and, looking back on it there were many, each congregation always produced at least one soul who was always loyal and always there. In Orkney it was Stanley. He was the verger. Stanley had a family of brothers and twin sisters, a mother, a wife and one small child and they were the backbone of St Olaf's. Anything that needed doing, Stanley was there, a constant support and unfailingly good-humoured. In Galashiels there was Mrs Hope, old by the time we got to know her, but always in church in the front seat in her black coat, indomitable, supportive, honest. Fortrose had Beattie who cleaned the church, lit the candles, opened the doors and attended every service, uncritical and undemanding, touchingly devout. Where times permitted she attended every other church service in the town too! In Baillieston there were the Macdonalds, Archie and Nessie. He was secretary to the vestry and she ran the MU, but they were so much more, a continual support and unfailingly good-tempered, gentle with their advice. I imagine every congregation has its Mrs Hope, its Beattie, its Stanley and its Macdonalds, the spiritual glue that holds the congregation together. When one dies there is always someone else, sometimes the most surprising person, to take over the role of dogsbody/ angel/server/saint. 'Boniface' if you like, the 'do-gooder'.

It was during John's ministry in Glasgow that I first came across the charismatic movement. I attended a service in St Mary's Episcopal Cathedral led by the Provost of the Cathedral of the Isles then known as the Collegiate Church of the Holy Spirit who had started a community inspired by the charismatic movement. He wore a flamboyant stole embroidered with the Holy Dove and there followed a lot of clapping, hands raised in prayer, unfamiliar hymns, weeping and shiny-eyed responses. For half a moment I felt the emotional tug, my own eyes almost filled with tears, but, at the same time, part of me was able to stand back and look at what was happening with amazement. I had been taught that emotions in church were untrustworthy, nor did I trust the extempore prayers which all seemed to begin with 'I just want to tell you, Lord....' Or, 'We just want to ask you, Father...' (what was 'just' about it?) Little that I could recognise or hold on to, and, in fact nothing I particularly wanted to tell or ask for either. However, one of the positive things I took away from that service was a beautiful modern hymn, 'song' as it was now called. *Lord Jesus Christ, You have come to us* thereafter became part of St Johns repertoire.

The charismatic movement formed its own organisation in Scotland, the Scottish Episcopal Renewal Fellowship, known as SERF. Nothing - or so it seemed to me - that had been done in the past was of much worth any more. It advocated 'renewal' in the form of Baptism in the Spirit, not forgetting 'speaking in tongues' which made no sense to my deaf ears, and anything the least out of the ordinary was pronounced 'a miracle!'. To declare however sincerely that, 'All you have to do is love Jesus,' is certainly true but to make it sound easy seemed to me like cheating. To be asked, 'Are you saved?' or 'Do you have a personal relationship with the Lord?' I found faintly embarrassing. I was once questioned by a young and eager journalist, 'Are you a Christian writer or are you a writer who happens to be a Christian?' I still don't know what she meant. I think that what makes me most uncomfortable is not just the eternal maty-ness and the shiny eyes of some charismatics, but the fact that many of those I met did not seem to recognise suffering, the appalling shame of Good Friday, the Christ that cried out in agony, 'My God, why have you forsaken me?' To tell an old friend of mine, a reserved and gentle Christian, whose husband was dying of a particularly nasty cancer that they had brought it on themselves because they had not truly loved the Lord Jesus was for me a particular blasphemy.

Fortunately John was not caught up with the fire, and fire it was that spread to many of the parishes. But it was also - unlike the burning bush - so often a transient fire. If a request for healing was not answered in the obvious way, the supplicant often gave up in despair. That was all too understandable, alas, but the exclusion of homosexuals and women priests from the ministry was not so easy to understand or excuse, the belief in the inerrancy of the Bible seemed to me to show ignorance. There are only two laws required of a Christian that I know of; to love God and to love your neighbour. Where does Christ ever say, 'Sorry, you're not welcome to serve my church because you're gay or because you're female?' He doesn't. Anywhere. Ever. To myself I had to say, sometimes through gritted teeth, Jesus also loves the charismatic movement. I suppose a part of me envied their fervour, their commitment and their un-embarrassment while at the same time I derided my own self-consciousness and awful desire to laugh at what seemed to me to be absurdities. I reckon that I had been inoculated with Christianity at my birth and was therefore incapable of ever catching that particular fire.

But I think that the stiff upper lip, unemotional approach to God in a society too embarrassed to mention his name is also mistaken. How can you say you love God and your emotions not be involved? Of course they are. How often have my eyes filled up during a particularly good sermon, or poured down my cheeks during the Three Hour Meditation on Good Friday or the hairs on my head lifted while the Ripon cathedral choir sang Allegri's *Miserere*. During my own wedding. quietly and hopefully unseen by most people, my eyes streamed. I remember Father Dennis and his 'gift of tears'. Of course you cannot love God without your heart. But it's only too easy for me to say there are only two laws required of me as a Christian; they happen to be harder to keep than all the rule books of the Old Testament put together. When I remember my unloving attitude in those days towards the charismatic movement, I am ashamed of myself. (Not enough, however, to join it.)

It was towards the end of John's ministry in Baillieston that I came to think seriously about gay ministry. Of course I had always known that there were as many shades of sexuality among the clergy as in any other walk of life and it had never bothered me. Indeed I had never given it more than a passing thought. That

162

some of the clergy were gay (queer was the horrid word used in those days) was a fact of life. So what? Then the Diocese of Glasgow appointed a gay bishop. That he had recently married someone in a wheelchair 'to look after her' was the perceived wisdom; 'how nice of him', the perceived response. John had arranged a Confirmation, quite a large one and it happened to be his last. The new Bishop wanted to visit us and would like to pray about it. We had a bit of a smile about that because we assumed that praying about it was part of his job. Anyhow, a date was fixed. He would come over for the afternoon, he would like to meet us both and then visit the candidates.

He arrived. I was completely wrong-footed to find he had straight longish brown hair swept off his face by a kirbygrip. A kirbygrip? I tried to not to stare too hard but I felt that dangerous bubble of laughter stirring in my throat. So I hurried away to make the tea.

After tea and cake and the usual polite conversation, John said, 'Would you bless us, Father?'

Taken by surprise I shot to my feet while John sank to his knees. The little bishop also stood. He reached up with one hand to touch my brow - I was about a head taller than him - and reached down with the other to touch John whose bald patch was very much in evidence. That bubble of laughter stirred dangerously but there was to be no escape. What followed was a long ramble, registering high on the charismatic scale. By the time it was over, I don't know who was the reddest, John from the hope, no doubt, that I would behave myself, me from the agony of holding the bubble back.

I didn't like that little bishop much but it was nothing to do with his campness (the kirbygrip I found rather endearing) or the fact that he was gay. It was his assumption that no one else but him and his fellow charismatics 'knew' the Lord Jesus. At least I presumed that was why he kept entreating the Holy Spirit that we might 'come to know the Lord Jesus'. The fact that he might be right did nothing for his popularity in St John's Rectory. I never knew what the candidates made of him.

Apart from Bishop Piers Holt Wilson, I never knew the many bishops that turned up annually to administer the sacrament of Confirmation all that well. Bishop James Lumsden Barkway of St Andrews from 1939-1949 who confirmed me was known in clerical circles as the 'slate pencil' because he was long and thin and grey. John was particularly fond of Fred Goldie of Glasgow who had served his home church in Dumbarton and Alastair Haggart of Edinburgh who had been his contemporary at Edinburgh Theological College. Francis Moncrieff, a tall cadaverous celibate, terrified me. Fred Easson of Aberdeen, a delightful companion, would spend about a week with us every year in Orkney in his travels round his diocese. Like me, he was a great cinema lover and we would always go together in Kirkwall during his visit whatever the film. He was kind enough to become Alison's godfather. If we had a particular favourite it had to be Duncan MacInnes, a Gaelic-speaking, genuine Episcopalian, who had been Chaplain to the Argyll and Sutherland Highlands, a POW and twice decorated for his war service. He was a truly lovable man. A bishop's life can't have been easy. I remember Kenneth Carey's overnight visits to Galashiels as particularly painful for he was not at his ease with women. But they were all decent good men available at the end of a phone to advise and pronounce on tricky parish situations as necessary. Bishops are one of the Church's better inventions.

So to come to the sixty-four dollar question (why sixty-four?). After a lifetime of parish life, do I believe any of it? God, the Trinity, the Church, the Resurrection, the Creed which I have repeated so often over the years that the words are almost meaningless.

First of all, God. Do I believe in God? Not all the time, no. I can't prove to you that God exists anymore than you can prove to me that he doesn't. However, if the word 'faith' implies doubt, then, yes, I have faith. There are times when I've thought to myself, it's all nonsense, wishful thinking, a primitive prop promising 'pie in the sky when I die'. Those were the times when I felt angry, out of sorts, ill-at-ease with my husband. Equally - no, not equally, far more often - I can truthfully say, 'Yes, I believe in you, God. Help my unbelief'. The more that science is able to unravel the mysteries of the universe the more I see God's hand in creation and in the making of mankind. God created the particle that became matter, and what amazing matter it is. An accident? No way. Haphazard? That is a ridiculous concept if you like. But 'the God of Everything', as Francis Spufford calls him, is not a person. God does not live in time. God is time, God is space, God is. Jaweh. 'I am'.

Then Jesus. I am a bit of a rebel when it comes to Jesus. Although I know he was a historical figure who lived and died on specific dates, I see the birth and resurrection stories as man's way of explaining the inexplicable and what wonderful metaphors they are. I don't believe that Jesus knew he was 'the only-begotten Son of God' right from early childhood. I believe it was revealed to him slowly just as it was revealed to him slowly that he was not only the Messiah of the Jews but also the Son of God for all mankind. But we are all sons and daughters of God, are we not? Apart from his incredible revelation of how the Kingdom of Heaven worked, apart from the extraordinary topsy-turvy fact of creator becoming created, what made Jesus so special? I believe God allowed himself to become man the more fully to understand the creature he had created and to experience, as a man, the nature of human love. I respect and admire and worship God, but I love Jesus. I love the fact that he could be gentle, he could be angry, he could get so tired that he could sleep through a storm, that he could weep, that he could be thirsty, that he liked a drink and fried fish, reach breaking point, love children...that he loves me. What makes Jesus so special is that he was/is as fully human as he is fully divine; that he can sit with me and walk with you and be on every altar and indeed at every table and every fireside at the same time is an entirely mind-blowing mystery and I do love a good mystery.

As for the Holy Spirit, I believe that I owe all that I am to it/him/her, all my enjoyment of life, the 'pizang', as Richard Burkitt calls it, of my own small creative talent. My Bird of Truth. When I look outward to find God, I see Jesus. When I look inward to hear God and listen to the voice that is always there inside me, prodding, warning, explaining, laughing at absurdities, I hear the Holy Spirit. I have never had any difficulty in accepting the concept of the Trinity. Another marvellous, unsolvable mystery that somehow makes such good sense.

The Communion of Saints is a comforting extension of God's love and care for mankind. There they all are, the souls of the departed, somewhere. I don't have to know exactly where and how. It is enough to know that they are present and that they too are experiencing Christ with us in the sacrifice of Communion. No one as yet understands dark matter but the scientists know that it exists. That's good enough for me. The Forgiveness of Sins is equally comforting. If we find falling out with a neighbour, a friend or member of the family unbearable, how much worse it is to fall out with God. We know that God doesn't like it either. Won't stand for it in fact. We know that from the most touching and revealing of all the parables, the Prodigal Son. Come to think of it, isn't that why Jesus died?

Do I believe in the Holy Catholic Church? Yes, I believe in my church in spite of its flaws, its pig-headedness, its absurdities. Above all, I love the prayer book, and in particular the Scottish Prayer Book of 1929. I own many prayer books from small Victorian tracts to modernised Benedictine missals. I have found something of value in most of them but in the end I always come back to the Scottish Prayer Book. Of all the liturgies and offices, I love Compline best with that string of night prayers each of which manages to say just what is necessary in the language of angels. Equally I love the psalms. I might pick out 121 which is sheer balm after a sticky day, or 139 which is such a comfort when other words fail.

And finally do I believe in the Resurrection and the Life Everlasting? A tough one, that. How often have I asked myself is it all wishful thinking? I admit I am a little scared when I think about the Life Everlasting. Do I really want life everlasting? All those different dimensions that the scientists talk about might possibly provide an answer but that explanation sounds just a little too pat, too simplistic, too man-made. On the other hand I cannot believe that all those millions of worlds that exist inside each one

166

of our heads are suddenly wiped out at death. What a waste. Nothing in nature is wasted, nothing lost. Our physical bodies are not wasted, 'dust to dust' so why should our souls, our persons be wasted by a God who has taken the trouble to create them? And what about Jesus? Whatever happened two thousand years ago, the truth is that hundreds of bystanders saw him die, others witnessed him buried and many more saw him alive again. Okay, it might have been a con trick but I cannot believe that the Jesus who was scourged, beaten and crucified was suddenly okay three days later. He would have been at death's door for weeks. Another mystery. How I love all these mysteries. It might all be a fearful shock what happens or doesn't happen next but I don't think so. I have high hopes for the future. We might find ourselves grinning with relief, happy to be home. 'Whew. Thank Goodness, that's over!'

What about hell? That place where Jesus visited before his resurrection? I certainly don't believe in the hell of fire and brimstone and endless torment. If God is the God of Everything then he is also the God of hell. If earth is a preparation for heaven, perhaps hell is another. I'm not afraid of hell.

So, hard though it is in so many ways to believe in the Creed and there have been times in my life when I've thought it all incredible, on the whole I find it harder not to believe. I don't have to understand. If we could understand God then we would be as God. I love that science unravels more and more of the wonders of the universe because each revelation is anther manifestation of that mystery.

Reading back on what I've written, do I make it all sound too cosy? Have I shown you my life through a pink lens? Possibly. Truthfully, it was never all that easy to be part of a parish family. I have known John come back from vestry meetings white and shaking. Sometimes he has brought back with him a fellow vestryman and plied him vicariously with the whisky he never drank himself. At one time when the Stewardship Campaign was causing friction he developed a temperature and had to go to hospital. The doctor diagnosed stress. Being such a superb organist himself, he had running battles with other organists over what seemed to me to be the most trivial matters.

I don't suppose it was ever easy to be a parish priest, because each member of a congregation has his or her own expectations of what a priest should do and no one man or woman can fulfil them all. Some have social skills, others have organisational skills, there are the committee men and there are the academics. Some preach superbly, others choreograph superb theatre in the sanctuary but can't string two sentences together. Looking at the adverts in the Church Times for parish vacancies, I smile a bit cynically to myself because all of them want the impossible. You cannot be all things to all people. If you try, you quickly become unstuck. So you have to be yourself, warts and all and only hope that with humility and the help of the Holy Spirit you don't clobber your own neck with too many millstones.

So, because this is my memoir, after reviewing the second third of my long life, I have to ask myself the final question, would I really have liked to be a priest? The answer is still yes, but this time it is a more hesitant yes, because in no way do I regret the life I had as a priest's wife nor the life that was to lie ahead of me for I was only in my mid-fifties when John retired in 1982 and the third part of my life was to take an unexpected turn. By 1994 when women were finally accepted into the priesthood. I believed I was too old to start again. I toyed with the idea of doing a course in theology but decided against it because by that time John was becoming frail and I was heavily involved in other commitments with books to write. I discovered that my best way of learning was by writing.

Within a fortnight of our removal back to the Black Isle I found myself with a museum to look after. I was to become immersed in a seemingly different world, that of our Pictish forbears. And yet in one way it was not so different. Pictish Christianity, as exemplified by the Cross-slab in Groam House so exquisitely carved with the symbols of Christ and the symbols of Pictland, is witness to the strong beliefs of our ancestors. This was a new joy, a new revelation of God's kingdom, and, for me, yet another delight. For the next thirteen years I was to live literally in the shadow of that Stone, the Soul of Rosemarkie. But that was for later.

I still think that of all vocations that of a priest's is the highest and thus possibly one of the hardest and getting harder as the decades go by for the devil no longer puts hunger, fame and power at the top of his list of temptations, he represents, quite simply, apathy. Christianity is just one big yawn to some, an embarrassment to others and an irrelevance to most. I should perhaps be grateful that the priesthood for me was never a possibility. I know I could never have measured up to the responsibility for the souls of a congregation, the daily repetition of the offices, the humility and the courage required to put on a clerical collar, walk down the street in a cassock, pray for a soul in crisis and be told to eff off. So no regrets then.

Come to think of it perhaps I had the best of all possible worlds. So what do you do when you've had a nice time? Say thank you. Thank you for so many things. For calling me to the life I had. Maybe it has not been full of excitements, wealth or adventure, but 'I have enjoyed every minute of it' as Jeanie V would say after a tea party. (Almost every minute.)

Thank you for the friends I have made over the years through school and university, writers groups, neighbours. Thank you for the congregations. I haven't always liked everyone, found it hard to find a reflection of the Creator in each person, but I appreciated the chance to get to know them, enjoyed their eccentricities and hope I haven't annoyed too many by my own.

Thank you for my family. For my birth family, my marriage and its amazing start and its still more amazing outcome. We - John and I - used to say to each other particularly towards the end of his life, how unbelievably blessed we have been in our children and in their children and their children's children. I know he's around somewhere keeping an eye open for us all, metaphorically jogging the arms of our guardian angels to look after those of us still in this world safe, sharing a special relationship with the ones who like him have also died. (Not 'passed' or 'past'. I cannot stand that euphemism)

And finally, if there can ever be an end to thanksgiving, to God himself in all his persons and aspects. So powerful that his universe is still expanding, so humble that he could lie in a manger, so generous that he allows us the freedom to make our own mistakes, so tender that he can weep over our follies, so forgiving that he will always take us back, so kindly that he can care about what happens to a sparrow, so loving that he could die so hideously for us. Thank you for the amazing gift of life. 'Yea verily' as the old Bible used to say. Yes, indeed.